A WHISPER OF GOD

Richard Clarke

A Whisper of God

ESSAYS ON POST-CATHOLIC IRELAND
AND THE CHRISTIAN FUTURE

First published in 2006 by
the columba press
55A Spruce Avenue, Stillorgan Industrial Park,
Blackrock, Co Dublin

Cover by Bill Bolger
Origination by The Columba Press
Printed in Ireland by Betaprint, Dublin

ISBN 1 85607 536 2

Acknowledgements
The author and publisher gratefully acknowledge the permission of the following to use material in their copyright: The Gallery Press for a quotation from *Collected Poems* by Derek Mahon; J. M. Dent, a division of the Orion Publishing Group, for a quotation from *Collected Poems 1945-1990* by R. S. Thomas.

Copyright © 2006, Richard Clarke

Table of Contents

Prelude	9
1. Doing Righteousness	13
2. A Question of Identity	22
3. Very Much Reality	31
4. Orders and Order	39
5. By What Authority?	46
6. Hope for Ideology	55
7. Coping with Culture – Niebuhr Revisited	65
8. Growing Unity	71
9. Mending Our Ways	76
10. Faiths and Faith	87
11. The Frontiers of Orthodoxy	97
12. All shall have Partners	109
13. Saving Victims	119
Postlude: Grace With Everything	129

For the foundations will be cast down: and what can the righteous do?
  – Psalm 11.3

  Let us be silent, so we may hear the whisper of the gods.
   – Ralph Waldo Emerson (Essay on Friendship)

Prelude

Surveying a terrain is not the same thing as traversing it, and nothing that follows in these essays will suggest any final or definite solutions to the task of the church as it faces the realities of a new, unfamiliar and decidedly alarming societal culture in the Ireland of today. It is also to a public *culture* I refer in my use of the term 'post-Catholic' as the sub-title for the essays. No disrespect is intended to the Roman Catholic Church; 'post-Catholic Ireland' is, as I will be suggesting, a new world for us all.

But there are, in any event, no final solutions to be found here. In the first place, the history of the 'final solution' is far from appealing but, secondly, the landscape of contemporary Irish culture – to continue the metaphor – seems at present to be more than a little prone to earthquake and seismic upheaval, and no definitive route map could ever expect to remain functional for an extended period of time. All that any of us may hope to do is to inspect the scenery as it is in reality, and then to suggest possible paths forward which may prove less ill-fated than the hapless alternative of standing still. The Irish church must somehow find the courage to leave behind, in a telling phrase of George Herbert, not only the gloomy cave of desperation but also the rock of pride. The church's pride and prestige has taken an extremely serious and thoroughly deserved beating in the events and revelations of these first years of the twenty-first century. It would therefore be more than tempting for it to dive into a cave of desperation and to aspire to nothing more than mere survival. But this would be the ultimate apostasy. We must take courage and move beyond the wreckage of past failures and infidelities.

But we must also move lightly for it is to God's whisper that we listen for guidance, rather than to the siren voices of quick fixes and applauded solutions. The voice of God will not be heard stridently and vehemently in Irish society today and this is the lesson the church must learn with no further delay. And we will make mistakes and miscalculations on our pilgrimage, but this is also as it must be. As the Ulster poet Louis MacNeice expressed it, with a characteristic jagged elegance in one of his poems, 'Entirely', 'in brute reality there is no road that is right entirely'. As he reminds us also in the poem, we might indeed be surer where we wished to go if the world were entirely black and white instead of being 'a prism of delight and pain', but we might also become merely bored and, in any event, those maps we require for forward movement are most certainly not always pristine or clear.

In the short essays that follow, I will use a terminology which may require some explanation at this point. I have long held that we should not speak of different Christian *churches*. In the words of the shared Christian credal statements there is indeed but 'one, holy, catholic and apostolic church', but within this one church there are different *traditions* – Roman Catholic, Anglican, Orthodox, Methodist, Presbyterian and others. There are indeed differences of style, attitude, ecclesiology, emphasis, and even of doctrine between (and within) the different Christian traditions and these cannot be overlooked or diminished. Nevertheless, by using the plural form of the word 'church', we are building false walls which are diplomatically but effectively degrading those who belong to a different tradition of Christianity than our own. I will therefore not be alluding to the different churches on the Irish scene, but to different Christian traditions. In places this may appear unwieldy – and for that I might almost apologise – but it is truly a matter of principle.

What is now attempted is a highly personalised collection of reflections on a future for the Irish church, less than systematic, but set out in hope rather than fear. As to whether what follows is focused on the church 'insider' or 'outsider', there may at times seem to be more than a little haziness. Perhaps the best answer is that it is directed slightly more towards the critical insider than the thoughtful outsider, although sometimes those two groups may have more in common than they sometimes imagine. What underpins all else however is the conviction that if the church in Ireland does not now practise the art of seeing itself as it is seen by those who are no longer part of it, its days as even a potential instrument of God's grace on this island are indeed numbered. This does not mean that God's presence and grace will still not be here in our midst and in a liberal abundance, but it will be rather that the institutional church has walked itself away from God. More than anything else, we must recover the God-given ability to listen to his whispered Word from the unanticipated source.

It was W H Auden who suggested that the gift of Pentecost may be as much the ability to hear God in unfamiliar language as to speak in strange tongues. In his remarkable late poem, 'Whitsunday in Kirchstetten', Auden found this extraordinary Pentecost gift a cause for rejoicing, as he attended the Whitsun mass in the local village church in Austria. He there discovered that 'we who were born congenitally deaf are able now to listen to rank outsiders'. The Holy Spirit does not in fact despise the golfer's eclectic vocabulary, the local Austrian accent, or even the sounds of Auden's 'own little anglo-american musico-literary set'. But on the other hand (as he also points out in this poem), our 'magic' spiritual language – in the light of the Holy Spirit – no longer has as much meaning as we might like to imagine, and even our treasured tribal religious mumbo jumbo is exposed by the Spirit for what it is.

It is not yet too late for the church to ask the forgiveness of God and of the people of post-Catholic Ireland for its congenital deafness. Nor may it be too late to allow our tribal formulae to be laid bare, however painful that may be, and to speak again of the love and power of God.

There is as little rhetoric or polemic in these pages as seemed practicable, but there will undoubtedly be moments when the writer's desire for the forceful may offend the reader's desire for decorum. For that, I am not certain that I should apologise. It may also seem that there is an undue reliance on poetry in these essays. This is somewhat difficult to explain, but it is certainly no affectation. Rather to my own surpise, I have found that it is only by a frequent recourse into poetry that any semblance of an overall focus may be maintained, and the temptation to relapse into a total imprecision of thought may – to some degree at least – be evaded.

I would like to thank the many people who have helped me in the construction of these essays, with their advice, support or valued companionship. In particular, I am grateful to my wife Linda who, on numerous occasions, has just encouraged me to 'keep at it'.

CHAPTER ONE

Doing Righteousness

The place where God most notably whispers in the scriptures is in a cave, and to Elijah.[1] There had been a great deal of noise directly before this incident, the splitting of mountains, the breaking of rocks, earthquake, tornado and fire. And there was much activity after this event, not least the handing over of responsibility to a new prophetic voice, that of Elisha. But the whisper of God was intrinsic to the grammar of prophetism. Only in quiet, with the listening, can the sound of righteousness be heard, in any world and at any time, and the truly righteous will always be the authentically prophetic.

It must of course be admitted that the word 'righteousness' (unlike 'prophetic') does have a distinctly unfortunate cadence in modern parlance. Perhaps this is because it appears to associate itself a little too readily with self-righteousness, both as a word and as a characteristic. It may also seem to suggest a definitive moral excellence or even perfection. But neither connotation is at all reasonable. In the biblical tradition, righteousness and self-righteousness have in fact nothing in common; they are polar opposites. (It was, I think, Pascal who observed that there are only two kinds of people, the righteous who believe they are sinners, and the sinners who believe they are righteous.) But neither does righteousness, certainly in the first instance, have quite as much to do with a stringent moralism as is usually taken to be the case. Righteousness, in both the Hebrew scriptures and in the New Testament, is about how we respond – in our living – to our relationship with God. This relationship with God is a covenant initiated not by us but by God, and an individual

---

1. 1 Kings 19.

is *righteous* when he or she is living out responsibly the obligations and requirements of this covenantal relationship. Righteousness thus has its only proper context in a relationship with God, and cannot be understood as abstract or individual virtue. And the righteous must therefore be – by definition – the very last people to be *self*-righteous. But they will be the first to be visionary.

In the New Testament, righteousness took on an entirely new dimension, whereby Jesus Christ came to be understood as embodying the entire righteousness of God. Christians were therefore called to become righteous, not through their own anxious efforts, but as incorporated into the life of Christ himself. Again, it was and is the relationship with God – God in Christ – which is primary, effective and paramount as the heart of all righteousness. True prophetic righteousness will secondarily have a connection with living uprightly, but this is within the corollary of righteousness, that the individual who seeks to respond with sincerity to the undeserved gift of *being in Christ* will not choose to live without moral restraint. But we may certain, before all else, that the righteous are still the strugglers and searchers; they are not those who imagine that they have finally accomplished and completed the business of righteousness.

When we then turn to the question of what the righteous are to do in a setting where so much of the societal foundation of the Christian faith appears to be in ruins, we are in fact asking how stumbling and flawed people who – despite their sense of inadequacy – seek nevertheless to connect their lives with God's, may connect constructively to the Irish culture of today. They must begin with silence, a troubled silence of reflection, of penitence and of stillness in which the whisper of God can be heard. When, after that silence, there is the whispered call to action, the encounter that follows will be prophetic, costly and radical. If righteousness is the working out in daily living of our engagement with a God who does not shout but whispers, then connecting those uncomfortable and often veiled truths of God with a surrounding society is an intensely demanding obligation on the righteous man or woman. But I begin the journey with some recent history and personal reflection.

The spring of 1967 was not a good time for the Church of Ireland. A distinguished English bishop, John Moorman, was invited to speak in Belfast Cathedral on the Second Vatican Council, at which he had been an Anglican observer. The Revd Ian Paisley, then growing in power and popularity in Northern Ireland, threatened street protests if this lecture were to go ahead. On the advice of the Royal Ulster Constabulary, the cathedral withdrew its invitation to Moorman. The Church of Ireland bishops of the time, although clearly disturbed, said very little that might be construed as critical of the decision by the cathedral authorities. As a teenager in Dublin, then about to leave school for university, it is no exaggeration to say that I was aghast. But then an article appeared in *The Irish Times*, written by the spirited Richard Hanson, then Professor of Theology in Nottingham University and within a few years to spend a brief and unhappy sojourn in Ireland as Bishop of Clogher. Hanson, Irish-born and ordained for the Church of Ireland, unreservedly savaged the leadership of the Church of Ireland. He referred them in particular to Dante, and to the third canto of *The Inferno*, where those who will not shoulder responsibility at a crucial moment are condemned to a state in the next life which is neither heaven nor hell, where they are disowned by everyone, and wander without direction while being eaten alive by insects. Hanson explained that 'the great refuser' in this passage of Dante is believed by some to be Pope Celestine V, who resigned papal office rather than take an unpopular stand. Other commentators see in that passage, understandably, the shades of Pontius Pilate who ritually washed his hands rather than defend or condemn Christ.

I now know a little more about Dante and a great deal more about the church, but Hanson's short prophetic article was undoubtedly a turning point within my own life. Not only was it one of the crucial urgings for me to explore further the matter of vocation to priesthood, but I began also to believe with new conviction that although one may make mistakes and there will indeed be times when initial reflection – attentiveness to the whisper of God – is necessary before decisive action, the refusal to shoulder responsibility when it is given to one, with the concomitant refusal to make a decision which must be made, is not only cowardly but truly depraved. This is not, however, the principal reason for the telling of this story. It is rather that, with every passing day, I believe more firmly that the Irish church – and by this I mean the wholeness of the Irish church and not any particular tradition within it – faces a Dantesque moment of truth in this opening decade of the twenty-first century. The Ireland in which the church is to do business has changed utterly. The church is now discredited and moribund in the eyes of many detached onlookers, but it must not therefore retreat into a frightened passivity concerned only with its own survival.

To adapt a celebrated image from the psalms, 'singing the Lord's song in a strange land' which is now Ireland will no longer draw applause. The song itself is mocked by many and the singing of it lustily may even draw down rough treatment on the singers. Even the song of justice is lampooned when it is associated with the voice of God. We can see clearly and repeatedly how those who, in the name of Christ, point to the appalling inequalities in Irish society are often shouted down or ridiculed as naïve. The calamitous temptation for the rest of us who lack their courage is that we will indeed sing that which is fashionable, obvious and already acceptable to all, but at a deeper level we will draw back from real controversy or any truly hazardous engagement with society. We would sooner do nothing than take any action we imagine might possibly make the church's current situation even worse. But to side with Dante's neutral angels, who in the battle between God and Satan refused to take any side, is infinitely more reprehensible than to make mistakes, even clumsy mistakes, in the honest pursuit of a renewed Christian proclamation. The Irish church of post-Catholic Ireland must begin to make hard and even dangerous choices about itself before it is too late, and with eyes wide open and

DOING RIGHTEOUSNESS

ears wider open still. It must listen, and with care. The voices around will be plentiful and raucous. The stillness and the whispering of the divine may be less discernible, but infinitely and eternally the more crucial.

My use of the term post-Catholic in these pages is hence both courteous and value-neutral. We are all part of post-Catholic Ireland, and this is what Ireland now is, as even the most sympathetic commentators within the Roman Catholic fold would agree. It is indeed an unfamiliar and puzzling world, but not only for the church. The poet Derek Mahon speaks sardonically of how, for the artist, the new freedoms given to the Irish backdrop have not been entirely advantageous.

What, in our new freedom, have we left to say?
Oh, poets can eat now, painters can buy paint
but have we nobler poetry, happier painting
than when the gutters bubbled, the drains stank
and hearts bobbed to the clappers in the sanctuary?
Has art, like life itself, its source in agony?
Nothing to lose but our chains, our chains gone
that bound with form the psycho-sexual turbulence,
together with those black hats and proper pubs,
at home now with the ersatz, the pop, the phony,
we seldom see a young nun, a copy of *An Phoblacht*
or love and hate, as once, with a full heart.
Those were the days; now patience, courage, artistry,
solitude things of the past, like the love of God,
we nod to you from the pastiche paradise
    of the post-modern.[2]

All of us must engage with new realities – social, aesthetic and religious. And those of us who care about the call to righteousness, and hence the summons to proclaim Christ in good times and bad, must finally learn to believe that a radical re-visioning – both spiritual and ecclesial – of the church as a

---

2. Derek Mahon, 'Shiver in your tenement', *Collected Poems*, The Gallery Press, 1999, p 230.

whole is essential if that proclamation is not to be further corrupted and ultimately destroyed. And it must therefore be a collective task, the shared project of all Christian people of goodwill on this island. Post-Catholic Ireland is, in other words, not merely a challenge for Roman Catholicism. The Ireland in which we live is a new place for everything that is Ireland. It is self-evidently a new environment for all the Christian traditions. It is revealing starkly the deep flaws in all of us. But it also offers authentic possibilities of 'making all things new' for the Christian project in its Irish setting.

There must therefore always be an absolute and absolutist *hope*, as we glimpse God's future for us. Although we cannot ignore our present and only too real experiences (both inside and outside the church) of sin, suffering and failure, the very foundation of the Christian gospel is that God's victory over death, evil and human failure has – in the only true dimension of reality – already been achieved in the death and resurrection of Jesus Christ. As Christians, as the righteous, we are placed in the world as it is, precisely for the purpose of confronting the forces of evil, darkness or indifference (and few things have more power than rank indifference) with those disturbing realities of a kingdom of God already victorious. These are realities which are perhaps more deeply disturbing for us than we ever wish to acknowledge, as we casually declaim our credal faith in a Christ who is not merely yesterday's influential man, but is God in Christ today and forever. The challenge for a righteous church (and we should never forget that the Hebrew scriptures in particular saw righteousness as an attribute of communities as much as of individuals) is to believe that we have been placed in this time and place, precisely for the God-given purpose of living amidst the realities of a post-Catholic Ireland.

In a rather neglected book within the Hebrew scriptures there is a remarkable scene when Queen Esther is confronted by Mordecai who challenges her to go to the King Ahasuerus and to intercede for her people, the Jews, who face annihilation. She is understandably terrified, as there is every likelihood that she will be executed for her insolence, particularly in view of the fact that executing the insubordinate is clearly a regular habit for Ahasuerus. The interchange between Mordecai and Esther is expressed with a particular grandeur in the *Revised Version* of the scriptures. To Esther's pleas to be relieved of her duties and to remain neutral, Mordecai responds,

> For if thou altogether hold thy peace at this time, then shall relief and deliverance arise for the Jews from another place, but thou and thy Father's house shall perish, and who knoweth whether thou art not come into the Kingdom for such a time as this? (Esther 4:14)

This is the austere challenge to Christians of today in post-Catholic Ireland. If the providence of God is to mean anything, it means that the believing Christians of today's Ireland have indeed been placed exactly where they are, precisely 'for such a time as this'.

One of the established maxims in the Judeo-Christian understanding of what constitutes a truthful and righteous life is a triad of demands in the Book of Micah in the Hebrew Bible, 'doing justly, loving mercy, and walking humbly with God'. But these three injunctions are often portrayed as three separate and distinct commands. Church and society in Ireland would do better to see them as belonging together. No-one can execute justice, while lacking a personal humility and genuine compassion. Nor can any individual or community walk with God and yet be indifferent to the solemn demands of justice and of compassion. And a sympathy which is patronising, or unconcerned with the underlying issues of truth and justice, is little more than posturing self-delusion.

In order to respond to this beckoning of providence in this time and place, the first demand placed upon us is surely the call of truth itself. In a prophetic sermon preached in Berlin in the early nineteen-thirties, just as Hitler was coming to power, Dietrich Bonhoeffer suggested that there are three 'knights of truth', the child, the fool, the sufferer.

The child tells the truth because he or she is unaware of the consequences of telling the truth. The child just tells things as he or she sees them. Any parent is aware just how embarrassing a child's total honesty can be as, in a piercing voice, he or she makes highly personal comments about visitors to the home within their hearing. This is truth told in innocence, even if a tactless innocence, but there is a freedom in such a truth.

Bonhoeffer's 'fool' is the fool in the mediaeval court, the court jester. The jester is more or less the only person who is allowed to tell the truth in that context. Nobody has to take him seriously, even though – deep down – everyone knows that he and he alone is telling the truth. The fool, the jester, is the only one who is free to tell the truth.

The 'sufferer' is the man who, as Bonhoeffer reminds us, is beaten and then tortured with a crown of thorns, who stands before Pontius Pilate and who is asked the ostensibly profound (but in fact deeply cynical) question by Pilate, 'What is truth'?... In his sermon, Bonhoeffer went on to suggest that what we are witnessing here is truth itself being crucified, and that it is Pilate who is judged by this crucified truth. Bonhoeffer then added a remarkable insight, telling us, almost as an aside, that *it is not we who ask for the truth, but the truth which asks for us*. This is the perspective the church is asked to put on its existence on this earth. It does not always seek the truth, it is often unable to face the truth, but in every situation the truth is seeking out the church. But this is not a strident truth. It is a whispered truth and at times an elusive truth, but always a definitive truth and one by which the church must submit to be judged.

The child and the jester are *free* in telling the truth. So was 'the sufferer'. Christ went to Calvary with more freedom than had Pilate who condemned him. Bonhoeffer died with more freedom than the millions of people who had enslaved themselves with Hitler's monumental untruth that the nation was more important than the gospel. And the truth of the gospel will never be found in giving people the answers they may want, solutions in national or racial superiority, relief in finding scapegoats for their desolation, or even in the economic miracle that

Hitler was to give them, but always at the cost of slavery, physical and spiritual.

The righteous of every age must live surrounded by truth and untruth. But, in every setting, the truth is asking for us. The truth offers freedom, whether the freedom of the young child for whom lies are just not part of the agenda, or of the fool who is known to be telling the truth even if people will not conform, or of the sufferer who is ready to take the awesome consequences of doing the truth. Sadly, we can avoid looking at the truth or hearing truth. We can too easily evade the truth that is asking for us. Truth does not speak loudly but softly. But truth and righteousness can belong nowhere if not to one another.

CHAPTER TWO

A Question of Identity

If we were ever to ask how Ireland would have been characterised for the entire twentieth century before its final decade, descriptions such as 'temperamentally rural', 'economically shaky', or 'self-consciously relaxed' might come readily to mind. But we realise that none of these portrayals might be easily applied to the Ireland of today. We do not expect that they will be applicable in the future either. Somewhere near the head of any list of characteristics of 'traditional' Ireland would also have appeared the description 'deeply religious'. And this is most certainly not a picture of Ireland in the opening years of the twenty-first century. But if we then decided to dig deeper into what we meant by religious, the notion of 'Catholic Ireland' would have quickly surfaced. This was a perfectly fair description, over a long period of time, of how Ireland understood itself and of how others saw it. To be fully Irish was to be a Roman Catholic. Not to be a Roman Catholic in Ireland (or at any rate a lapsed Roman Catholic) was to be less than fully Irish and, quite possibly, to have at least a slight antipathy to Irish independence. Roman Catholic and non-Roman Catholic alike for the most part lived out this story of identity and non-identity on the island of Ireland, and if we are therefore to speak sensibly of post-Catholic Ireland it would be helpful to unpack – however briefly – what Catholic Ireland may have been. From this perspective, it is certainly of use to think of Catholic Ireland as being – in some sense at least – a socio-political phenomenon, one 'age' among many in the span of Irish history.

Some of what follows may indeed make contentious reading; many of the judgements may appear abrasive, but nothing here is judgemental. It is surely only when we are all realistic about ourselves and where we have come from, and are truthful about the stories we have told ourselves and others, that we may move forwards together in the providence of God. The Nigerian writer, Ben Okri, gives us some incentive in the matter:

> Nations and peoples are largely the stories they feed themselves. If they tell themselves stories that are lies, they will suffer the future consequences of those lies. If they tell themselves stories that face their own truths, they will free their histories for future flowerings.[3]

And, within the same exegesis on the importance of being ruthlessly honest about our stories, Okri gives even more trenchant advice to the Irish church of today:

> There are many ways to die and not all of them have to do with extinction. A lot of them have to do with living. Living many lies. Living without asking questions. Living in a cave of your own prejudices. Living the life imposed on you, the dreams and codes of your ancestors.[4]

Catholic Ireland as such – the casual identifying of *real* Irishness with membership of the Roman Catholic Church – may be dated more or less from the mid-nineteenth century until the end of the twentieth century. In terms of numerical membership, Ireland was of course predominantly Roman Catholic well before the mid-nineteenth century, in that the reformed traditions have never been more than a numerical minority on this island. But the reality of Catholic Ireland was something more psychologically ingrained than a mere numeric strength. In the first place, it simply did not exist before the 1850s. Ideas of any type of *nationhood*, as we would understand nationhood and nationalism today, were still in a process of evolution through the early part of the nineteenth century. Irish-ness simply could not have carried the narrow nationalistic connotation it would later come to hold. It should be added that, until the late nineteenth

---

3. Ben Okri, *A Way of Being Free*, Phoenix Books, 1997, p 112.
4. ibid, p 5.

century, earlier Irish separatists such as a Wolfe Tone, Robert Emmet, Henry Joy McCracken or Thomas Davis were allowed their rightful place within the Protestant culture of their birth, rather than being regarded either as renegades to their origins or as honorary Roman Catholics. History had moved into the era of the Protestant nationalist Charles Stewart Parnell before that all was to change.

We may do well to accept also that Catholic Ireland was, in part at least, a political creation. The recognised involvement of the Catholic Church with the Nationalist Association in the mid-nineteenth century was partly a strategy to attract faithful Roman Catholics away from the extremes of Fenianism into a more moderate form of Irish nationalism. This could only be done if support for Irish nationalism were seen as part of the basic identity of any good Roman Catholic on the island of Ireland. There were undoubtedly other agendas in operation as well. Cardinal Paul Cullen saw part of his mission as being to bring the Catholic Church in Ireland, which had a long tradition of independent-mindedness, into a closer relationship with Rome. This also would be better achieved if the increasingly unifying force of Irish nationalism were harnessed to a religious identity, rather than remaining within a purely political context.

There was nothing particularly shameful or cynical about any of this. If *Catholic Ireland* was in part an intentional stratagem, the story was also a natural development from a situation where the membership of all the reformed Christian traditions on the island (and in particular the Church of Ireland) was becoming ever more distrustful and apprehensive of a future Ireland which would be politically independent of Britain. Inevitably, cultural reaction and counter-reaction consolidated the perception that Irish-ness and Catholicism were all but coterminous in the life of the island. *Unionism* and *Protestantism*, particularly in the province of Ulster, but in effect throughout the island, became an increasingly effortless elision. None of this has proved wholesome for the history of Ireland.

In Northern Ireland, it was an insult to the entire liberal

democratic tradition of western Europe that the phrase 'A Protestant parliament for a Protestant people' could even be uttered, let alone accepted by so many with apparent approval. In southern Ireland, both during its earlier manifestation as the Free State and in its first decades as a Republic, it was utterly shameful that any citizens might feel (as many did) that they were somehow not quite as fully people of the land of their birth as were their Roman Catholic neighbours. Nothing except the cause of atheism truly profited, as religious sectarianism – whether open and strident, or genteel and whispered – overran the entire island.

Many within the reformed traditions, particularly in Ulster (and not merely the entity of Northern Ireland) have learnt a cruel lesson. Having given sustenance and encouragement to the 'loyal orders' – largely in order that the Protestant flock might be more effectively corralled – there was a bitter harvest to be reaped. During the late twentieth century conflict in Northern Ireland the loyal orders felt (and not unreasonably) that they were now entitled to a reciprocal loyalty from those Protestant church communities which in previous generations had given them such open support. The inevitable corollary was that the strange détente between Roman Catholicism and Irish identity throughout the island became ever more problematical, as moderate nationalism and fervent republicanism each sought to establish its own hegemony over the hearts and minds of Catholic men and women. There is much for which virtually every major Christian tradition on this island should feel acute shame, as it surveys the ways in which the story has unfolded, and the menacing sectarian effects of the over-association of its individual confessional stance with a particular national identity, whether of green or orange hue. As T S Eliot edgily reminded us in his poem 'East Coker', we should not be impressed by the supposed wisdom of old men but remember instead 'their folly, their fear of fear and frenzy, their fear of possession, of belonging to one another, or to others, or to God'. There is in fact only one wisdom to acquire, says Eliot, and this is the wisdom of humility, which is endless.

We cannot therefore deny the story thus far, nor can we honourably distance ourselves from the tale as it unfolded. We can, however, face up to its consequences and resolve humbly to be transformed into a new identity. This can only be an identity which releases itself gently from the baggage of its inheritance, without reproach and without the compunction to score points over the erstwhile foes and rivals. The throwing of stones receives no commendation from the gospel of Christ. Perhaps when we succumb to the temptation to criticise or condemn, we should hear the words of that peace-loving Israeli, Yehuda Amichai, echoing gently and whimsically in our ears. Only thus will the story of the identity of the Irish church ever be transfigured.

Please do not throw any more stones,
You are moving the land,
The holy, whole, open land,
You are moving it to the sea
And the sea doesn't want it
The sea says, not in me.

Please throw little stones,
Throw snail fossils, throw gravel,
Justice or injustice from the quarries of Migdal Tsedek,
Throw soft stones, throw sweet clods,
Throw limestone, throw clay,
Throw sand of the seashore,
Throw dust of the desert, throw rust,
Throw soil, throw wind,
Throw air, throw nothing
Until your hands are weary
And the war is weary
And even peace will be weary and will be.

Many stones have been thrown by the church. Many stones are now being thrown at the church.

There are many sociological causes for the swift shift from Catholic Ireland to post-Catholic Ireland. Much has been made of the impact of the exposure of a large number of child abuse cases involving Catholic clergy through the nineteen-nineties. Undoubtedly this caused a massive loss of confidence in the Catholic Church as an institution. It gave credence to those who had long resented and despised the church. It showed up reluctance within the leadership of the church to risk the reputation of the institution in order to deal rigorously with those who had disgraced their calling. Yet, had all been well in every other aspect of the life of all the Christian traditions, this loss of reputation might have been overcome. But much else was going awry. Catholic Ireland, in the form in which it was known (and in which it reached its apogee in the years before the Second Vatican Council) would have been eroded regardless of those revelations of child abuse. The primary offence of the whole church, and certainly not the Roman Catholic tradition alone, was to believe that it was somehow above and beyond accountability, perhaps even an accountability to God himself. For many years, virtually all the mainstream Christian traditions in Ireland had basked in their shared position of privilege and status in the life of the country. One must in fairness, I believe, note an honourable exception here in the Methodist tradition which (although at times inordinately proud of its specifically Wesleyan inheritance) has never sought much place in the social or political sun. Its strong emphasis, in keeping with its nineteenth century development in the working classes of Britain, was on social inclusiveness and on making the church a place of welcome to all, regardless of rank or style. That having been said, the mainstream Christian traditions in Ireland did for the most part take for granted their position in public esteem and on the public stage, and there has been a strong element of hubris in the fall from grace. In that fall, God is to be found. God is murmuring again that the blessed are those who are without worldly power and prestige.

There was indeed an intensely worldly assumption that the churches would for ever be hand in glove with the instruments of government, north and south. Those in government were, for a surprisingly long time, more than content to sustain this bond. In the Irish setting today, however, for any tradition to oppose a particular public policy with vehemence would be no guarantee of receiving a hearing from government, let alone influencing any change in that policy. No political party in Ireland any longer needs even the tacit approval of the church in order to gain power or to remain in power. Politics throughout Ireland, north or south, simply does not need the church in the way it once did. We might indeed go further and suggest that to have enthusiastic backing from any church tradition might today even be an electoral liability for a political party. Times have indeed changed, although the church has been somewhat slow in recognising this.

If the Irish church can no longer hector the powers of the state, it still hankers after a place in the corridors of power. The certainty is that it will entirely lose its Christian bearings if it nourishes the vain hope of retaining its identity in some tacit but visible connection between itelf and political power in this land. The church might indeed continue some form of existence along this road but only as a toadying chaplain to the predominant political parties of the particular day. We should never forget the wisdom of Camus in suggesting that from the time of Saint Paul to that of Stalin, the popes who have chosen Caesar have prepared the way for the Caesars who quickly learn to despise popes.

The freedom which, as the founder of Christianity warns us, is always allied to truth cannot be an easy freedom. It is not the freedom to luxuriate in privilege or status. But there is undeniably a true Christian freedom which comes from knowing that it is God's grace rather than worldly recognition or prominence which will save the church. There is a freedom in accepting that the church must face the nation with honest penitence rather than in mendacious pretence. The person who has been 'found out' has a greater freedom than those who continue to pretend that they are above reproach or criticism. A church which is prepared to come out of its corroding bunker with its hands up may yet regain the trust of the people of post-Catholic Ireland. Humility need not necessarily obviate purpose or determination. George Herbert points to a crucial balance:

Pitch thy behaviour low, thy projects high;
So shalt thou humble and magnanimous be:
Sink not in spirit: who aimeth at the sky,
Shoots much higher than he that means the tree.
A grain of glory mixt with humbleness
Cures both a fever and lethargicness.[5]

If in a new-found vulnerability and humility the church were to heed God's undertones, it will quietly learn the difficult lesson that it is not only those who are religious who really know about God. God does not need our religion in order to be God. God is not the possession of the church, nor does God care only for the religious; indeed the gospels would rather suggest that Jesus cared less for the religious than for those who were far from religious. Nor, for that matter, is God to be found only in or behind our structures and sacred spaces. He does not speak only where or how the church allows him to speak. The good news of the incarnation is that God is openly and even shockingly alive in the very places where religious people do not think he should be. The more the righteous of the church seek to regard God as an object who is to be made relevant to others, the more God will evade their church. What the church can offer to the world is not a religion 'that works' nor even a God whom we can offer to others within our structures and ceremonies, but a God who in Christ has taken hold of us, and who is fully and even preposterously at large in the world of post-Catholic Ireland, not because the church has put him there, but very often *despite* the follies, self-delusion and self-aggrandisement of the church. Whether or not the world wants him or recognises him, God is within this world and this culture, even at its most antagonistic and religiously careless. He is to be found in the anti-clericalism from which the institutional church shrinks in fear.

---

5. George Herbert, 'The Church Porch', *The Complete English Works*, Everyman's Library, 1995, p 18.

To suggest that God can disclose himself only within the religious structures is to surrender the incarnation to the religion of the gnostics, the religious insider dealers of the early church who believed that God could disclose himself only to those who had their particular in-house specialist knowledge of him. The gnostics are still among us, but their god is not the God of righteousness.

CHAPTER THREE

Very Much Reality

Within the Irish church, there has been an undoubted presumption that the tenets of the Christian faith, and a deep-seated allegiance to the individual religious tradition of one's birth, were givens which would never be challenged on any large scale by those who had grown up 'within the faith'. The illusion developed that even if young people became a little slack about their involvement in the church, they would almost certainly return to the ecclesiastical fold as soon as they had settled down, happily married – ideally – to a member of the same religious tradition. There was an astonishingly belated awareness on the part of the church that, as Ireland became less insular, and continental Europe became a more familiar place (particularly for those living in the Republic of Ireland), there would be fewer and fewer givens of any kind, religious, political or social. In many respects, however, the differing evolutions of Northern Ireland and the Republic have meant that religion itself does not mean the same thing in each.

Northern Ireland, enduring as it did the traumas and suffering of thirty years of political violence, has inevitably become more introspective than the Republic. Continental Europe (and, ironically, even mainland Britain) were not familiar places, particularly to an older generation in Northern Ireland. For many years of 'the troubles', a large number of the young people who had left Northern Ireland for university education in Britain did not return to Ireland, north or south. Religious change may have happened, but it was not over-connected to an exposure to international culture.

On the other hand, as travel and the opportunities for travel became financially and socially more manageable, the Republic found itself less and less isolated from the modes and fashions of a wider world. A more *laissez-faire* attitude to religious faith, encountered in Britain or Europe, inevitably had its influence. Greater mobility meant that that young people (and, indeed, the not so young) were no longer chained, metaphorically or geographically, to a single locality for a lifetime. And so the familiarity of the faith as encountered in the local community was no longer a natural part of a rhythm of life to take one from cradle to grave. A generation of young people, who were now being educated to levels never before contemplated as the normal expectation for the majority, would need to be energetically persuaded that the Christian faith was either credible or desirable. With a few impressive exceptions, the different church traditions did not even see this challenge, let alone rise to it.

Again, the different Christian communities did not – for the most part – see the under-side of Irish society. As community itself throughout Ireland became ever more fractured, there were those who had no community of any kind to sustain them. They had become dross on the streets of the cities, and few others noticed, unless it was to complain about higher levels of violence or dirt. God's essential presence with the dispossessed and the down-and-out remained unobserved and unheard. If we leave aside the brave and prophetic few, the church as an institution (in all its traditions) continued to live within a comfortable delusion that all was reasonably well, and that the Christian church was held in high regard by all right-thinking people, even by those who no longer attended worship.

The Greeley-Ward survey on religious attitudes in Ireland – reported in *Doctrine and Life* in December 2000 – suggested that many people who otherwise had little time for the church nevertheless retained a respect for their local priest. One should never contradict any survey with personal observation but one is left wondering if, even a very few years later, the respect of the churched (let alone the rapidly increasingly constituency of the unchurched) for the clergy not now is less certain. In fact the recent European Values Survey and European Social Survey (correlated in *Conflict and Consensus*,[6] published in 2005) suggest that public trust in the church *per se* is now at a far lower level, even among church goers. The incidence of regular churchgoing is certainly dropping fast, but not even those who attend church services regularly would necessarily 'trust the church'. Only 29% of regular Roman Catholic church attenders in the Republic of Ireland claimed to have a great deal of confidence in the church; the figure for 'Protestant' churchgoers in the Republic was slightly higher (at 42%), and in Northern Ireland the figures were higher for both Roman Catholics and Protestants. But no-one who cares for the church within any of its traditions need take comfort from the findings. In no category of church-goer did the figure rise above fifty percent for those who admit to having a great deal of trust in the church, and it must again be emphasised that we are speaking here only of those who still attend church regularly.

Not surprisingly, the downward shift in public esteem has had its effects on the institutional life of the different church traditions. It is seen very clearly in the numbers of those wishing to be ordained. The individual acceptance of a vocation, which in most of the churches would have been seen in a previous generation as honourable and reasonable for a young person, is fast being seen as at best an eccentricity, even within the active life of the different Christian traditions themselves. But this state of affairs did not begin in the nineteen nineties. It had been developing over at least two decades. In the Church of Ireland (as within the Roman Catholic Church also) it is many years since it was seen almost as a badge of honour to have 'a priest in the family'. And, as the ordained became fewer in number, and as the appearance of the average priest took on a more elderly aspect, the attractiveness of the ordained ministry as a vocation for a young person became less apparent. There is of course an obvious vicious

---

6. Tony Fahey, Bernadette C Hayes, Richard Sinnott, *Conflict and Consensus – A study of values and attitudes in the Republic of Ireland and Northern Ireland*, Dublin: Institute of Public Administration, 2005.

circle at work here, particularly in a society traditionally used to a high visible profile of the church. The less visible the priesthood (and the more elderly that priesthood), the fewer will be those drawn naturally to priesthood as 'a good thing to be'. The less visible the church as a whole, the less obvious will seem the basic faith claims on which the church is based. Year by year, there are fewer clergy working in parishes and, inevitably, there is a less personal relationship between the committed church family and the harassed and over-worked pastor, of whatever tradition. The priest is today not the commonplace and accepted part of the landscape he once was, no longer as natural, in Patrick Kavanagh's phrase, 'as a round stone in a green field'.

Eliot's poetic comment that 'it is hard for those who live near a police station to believe in the triumph of violence' may readily be applied to the visibility of the church and its ordained functionaries. It is somewhat easier to believe in the existence of God when the church and all its observable externals are on constant view all around you. It is harder to accept the fundamentals of the faith uncritically, when the visible signs of the institutional church are disappearing before your eyes. Vocations to ordination in the Roman Catholic Church have nose-dived in recent years. The Church of Ireland has fared a little better, but the proverbial supply is not meeting demand, and within this tradition the ordination of a man or woman in their mid-twenties is today very much the exception rather than the rule.

Perhaps more surprisingly, the public posture of those who have abandoned their practice of religion appears to be in considerable contrast to the position in the England of today. Involvement in the life of the Church in England is very much a minority pursuit. The numbers of those attending Christian worship with any regularity in England is lower than for many generations and is still plummeting. There has, however, remained a residual respect for what the church as a whole may stand for, even if there is little sign of any widespread commitment to the Christian faith. Clergy in clerical collars are, for the most part, free to walk the streets of English cities without fear of abuse or violence, something which cannot now be said for the cities or towns of the Irish Republic. In Britain there is certainly a mockery of the stranger foibles of the church (and of the Church of England in particular), but it is not for the most part a pitiless contempt. One may still read reflective articles on faith – including some written by complete non-believers – in the broadsheet British press. Chattering Ireland, on the other hand, appears to be moving swiftly from a mood of antagonism to the church, to a new attitude of sneering dismissal of the Christian faith itself. There is new currency in Ireland for the notion that few within the church – even within its ordained ministry – really believe in Christianity anyhow, and that the entire apparatus of the church is founded on intentional hypocrisy or infantile escapism. The implication is that the Christian message is not truly believed, even by those who preach it. There is indeed a growing and merciless cynicism in post-Catholic Ireland not merely towards the unattractiveness of the church (which might be perfectly understandable), but even towards the Christian faith that underpins the church's existence.

This has inevitably caused a crisis within the church, and within all its traditions. Perhaps the first indication of pain is in a lowering of confidence now apparent among at least some clergy. A culture of unease and insecurity has inevitably infected morale within the ordained ministry of the whole church, in an Ireland where vocation to ordained ministry – in whatever tradition – now appears to many in society as an act of pitiable hypocrisy or as an indication of psychological inadequacy. There is no longer an honoured place given to the priest, minister, religious brother or sister in the culture of Irish post-Catholic society.

An unease among the ordained manifests itself within different age-groups in differing ways. Statistically, many more now leave the ordained ministry at an early stage than would have been the case a generation ago. In the Roman Catholic context, this has sometimes been over-casually attributed to the demands of priestly celibacy, but it is a feature in Church of Ireland life also, and this would certainly suggest that a notable discomfiture within the ordained ministry has a more general origin. At a later stage in life, many of the clergy of today appear to be struggling harder than in a previous generation against the twin dangers of burn-out and cynicism, or indeed a combination of both. The prospect of retirement for many resembles more a foretaste of heaven than an unfortunate necessity engendered by the infirmities of old age.

Moving from the ordained ministry in particular, it must be concluded also that many people – and not merely the young – have seemingly decided that their belief was in fact more a conformity to social convention than to an individual commitment of faith, and have simply discarded the church. But for others there has been a movement towards what might best be expressed as *ghetto church*. By this I mean the retreat behind the security of a metaphorical ghetto wall, separating church life from the outside world, in effect a world of reality. Were Christian disciples to follow this path – separating their church involvement from all else around – the church might indeed survive, smaller but more cohesive. It would become an institution for those who are attracted to it, who would give to it an unconditional loyalty with one area of their lives, and who would maintain it financially. If this retrenchment were to become a widespread response, the church might indeed endure (and for quite some time) in many parts of the island, albeit with ever diminishing numbers. But it would most certainly assume the appearance of a private club for those who like religion or who find it therapeutic. The likelihood is that it would not be persecuted by those who were not part of it. It would simply be ignored as irrelevant by most of the society around it. As the ghetto grew smaller it would almost certainly become even more exclusive and extremely conservative. The insiders would hark back wistfully to a non-existent golden age of the church, when certainties were accepted without question. It would become ever more hierarchical – even if not in name – and its leadership ever more defensive and authoritarian. The rules of the club would become more restrictive and intolerant. At this stage the ghetto church would begin to fragment into smaller ghettos, each convinced that it alone was the only faithful remnant, and that it alone was preserving the fulness of Christian truth. This would be no place for the troubling whisper of God but only for the belligerent certitude. Far from being the fanciful and exaggerated scenario for an unlikely future, we surely see within all our traditions a steady progression – if that is what indeed is – in the direction of ghetto church.

Even before we reach the outskirts of the ghetto church, there are indications of fissuring, within every Christian tradition, into 'conservative' and 'liberal' factions. This may be attributed entirely to new and deep-seated insecurities within today's church. Divisions within Christian traditions are of course nothing new, but within each faction there is a new intensity of conviction that those who feel and speak differently must lack either integrity or intelligence or – indeed – both. What we may indeed be witnessing today is a state of affairs whereby the traditionalists of one Christian tradition are finding that they have more in common with fellow conservatives of other traditions than with those of their own tradition who now seem to them to be dangerously at variance with the gospel. And the same may be said, *mutatis mutandis*, with equal certainty for the liberals, radicals, or any other grouping within each tradition.

Much of what has been outlined briefly here may seem unduly pessimistic. It may seem exaggerated, and perhaps it is. But until the Christian church of post-catholic Ireland, in all its traditions, will face the unpalatable truth that the past is not there for retrieval, there is little hope for the Christian task. The uncomfortable truth is, as has already been noted, that the Irish state no longer needs the approval of the church. There are many good people who believe, and not without reason, that all religion leads to violence and hatred. And, within the church, a residual uncritical loyalty is all but dead. For many who do not find the church repellant, it is merely a total and yawn-inducing irrelevance. No plethora of vapid episcopal pronouncements and statements on everything under the sun will change that situation. It is an unassuming persuasiveness, not the megaphone, sound-bite or truncheon, which will enable people to see that the light of Christ may yet be found within the institutional church. We may also take it as axiomatic that a country which finds the church unsavoury will never take seriously a self-proclaimed 'Body of Christ' which is content to operate as a series of competing businesses; a far greater unity of purpose between different traditions is not merely a desirable option, it is an imperative. The church – as One, Holy, Catholic and Apostolic Church – can now commend Christ or itself to post-Catholic Ireland only by the attentiveness and unitedness of its God-centred inner life, and by an equal attentiveness and unitedness in its self-giving to the world.

CHAPTER FOUR

Orders and Order

Having established that God does not actually need the institutional church (in that God would remain God without the church and his presence is already to be found in places where the church is loath to utter his name) an honest question must sooner or later be faced as to whether ordained clergy are a humanly devised (and hence expendable) structure or are a God-given essential for a church which wishes to do realistic business with a world which neither knows nor much cares what clergy are, and which is indeed not over-fond of them as a species anyhow.

We may certainly say that, in its mainstream traditions, the Christian Church has from earliest times authorised a particular ministry permitted to do specific 'church-things' which other members were not authorised to do, presiding at the eucharist in particular. The authorisation or ordination of these individuals was more than a local arrangement and carried with it a universality and hence, in every sense, a catholicity. This may indeed be an essential, if any sense of a universality of church or eucharist (or sacraments in general) is to be retained – in other words, if the local church community is to be more than just local, but is to have an identity in a wider reality of the Catholic Church. Its baptism, eucharist and ordained ministry can only be connected with the church outside the local community if it is has in some way been authorised and 'ordered' by the whole church.

That having been said, we then have to consider whether the way the church has used its ordained ministry is of the essence of that ministry. We now think instinctively of the ordained minister as a person apart. In order to minister to community, it seems to be taken for granted that he (or she) must have an elemental separatedness from the community. A sense of separatedness and loneliness is vividly captured by a poet priest, R S Thomas, in his poem 'The Priest':

> The priest picks his way
> Through the parish. Eyes watch him
> From windows, from the farms;
> Hearts wanting him to come near.
> The flesh rejects him.
>
> Women, pouring from the black kettle,
> Stir up the whirling tea-grounds
> Of their thoughts; offer him a dark
> Filling in their smiling sandwich.
>
> Priests have a long way to go.
> The people wait for them to come
> To them over the broken glass
> Of their vows, making them pay
> With their sweat's coinage for their correction.
>
> He goes up a green lane
> Through growing branches; lambs cushion
> His vision. He comes slowly down
> In the dark, feeling the cross warp
> In his hands; hanging on it his thought's icicles.
>
> 'Crippled soul,' do you say? Looking at him
> From the mind's height; 'limping through life
> On his prayers. There are other people
> In the world, sitting at table
> Contented, though the broken body
> And the shed blood are not on the menu'.

'Let it be so,' I say. 'Amen and amen.'[7]

A separatedness, in the sense of some degree of necessary objectivity and detachment, is undoubtedly a concomitant within

---
7. R S Thomas, *Collected Poems 1945-1990*, J M Dent, 1993, p 196.

any calling to minister to others – in any 'profession' as in the ordained ministry – but there is no doubt that the perception of the priest as a separate caste has not always been the understanding of priesthood in the church. Before Reformation times, the priest in a local setting would have been regarded as akin to a tradesman, very much part of and within his community. There were certain things which the priest did in and for the community, things which he was allowed to do and which were only his to do. His was the business of baptising and massing. Ideally he would be good at caring for the people. He might not be particularly learned – one looked to the religious orders for learning and theology – but he was, hopefully, a good man within the community who said his prayers, and who did the priest functions. In Chaucer's admittedly idealised picture (in the Prologue to *The Canterbury Tales*) the true priest was poor and unambitious, he stayed at home and cared for his parishioners, so that no wolf would cause them to be led astray. Above all else, he belonged to the community as a pastor rather than a hired mercenary.

It has been only since the Reformation that the priesthood has tended to become – with a greater emphasis on the distinctiveness, the personal holiness and the requisite skills (in particular the theological learning) of the priest, and an attendant insistence on seminarian separatedness in formation – a sacred caste within the church. With an enforced celibacy (which would have been less than rigid *de facto* in many places during the late mediaeval period), this separatedness may appear to be more marked in the Roman Catholic tradition than in others, but it is in reality a discernible feature within all the mainstream western Christian traditions. Most priests, clergy and pastors – married or unmarried – could at times identify with R S Thomas' isolated priest. Interestingly and significantly, the perception of being inherently separated from community appears to be far less evident in the Orthodox tradition of priesthood, which seems to accord more closely to the more comfortable and community integrated picture of the western 'mediaeval' priest as described earlier.

If church and society have changed the *appearance* of priest in relation to community, and if we can accept that this appearance is not the quintessence of priesthood, where then is the core of priesthood? Is it only in fulfilling specified functions for the church (largely sacramental but also pastoral) or is it to be more? Ordination in the Catholic understanding (and here the word 'Catholic' is used in its fullest sense) is always understood as being the call of God *and* the call of Church to specific ministry. Ordination to priesthood is seen as having both a vertical and a horizontal dimension, but it is the former which precedes and transcends the latter. The elemental call, being from God, means that God does effect more than a functionistic change in the weak, shallow, vain and flawed human being whom he has called. This does not make the individual *better* than anyone else in the Christian community. It should not carry of itself any prestige other than a sense of the strangeness of God's grace and, one would hope, a gratitude for that grace. But, held into a tension with this, is surely the reality that a priest or pastor operates within community, and only with the support and trust of that community. From earliest Christian times, the consent of the people was required before an ordination could proceed. There were many cases in the history of the early church (before institutional centralisation was the predominant feature of church life it quickly became) where an individual was acclaimed bishop by a local Christianity community, and where this local acclamation gave the ordination a validity which the whole wider church would then recognise. The call for the consent of community is still to be found within modern ordinals, but it has become (one has regretfully to admit) rather more a symbol than a genuine moment of truth. A priest is what God has made him or her at ordination, but priesthood must also be recognised, confirmed and validated by what priests do. In the post-modern world of post-Catholic Ireland, we have to admit that many people – even within the church – do not even begin to grasp the notion.

The church today must therefore be ready to proclaim with

proper confidence that it is not just humans but God who makes people priests at ordination; it is not only the church but God who puts his hands on them. This image of God *putting his hands* on his pastors is part of a phrase used by a character in Alan Paton's famous novel, *Cry the Beloved Country*, set in the injustices and hatreds of the South Africa of fifty years ago. A friend of the main character in the novel, Stephen Kumalo, is another pastor, Theophilus Msimangu. At one moving point in the story, Msimangu explains himself and what he is; he doesn't see himself as good, far from it, but he recognises what his call from God meant and continues to mean. He says gently to Kumalo in one of the pivotal points in the novel, 'I am a weak and sinful man, but God put His hands on me, that is all.' Perhaps that is all that needs to be said about ordination itself, but all ministry is to be rooted firmly in a theology of God and a theology of baptism. It is not about clergy using their influence and power to keep the laity satisfied and occupied within the ambit of the church.

For centuries, the ordained ministry in the western traditions has been understood in terms of power. Indeed the ordained ministry was perceived as the summit of all Christian ministry, if not the totality of what was meant by ministry. Gradually attitudes have changed and the term 'ministry of the laity' has become more than a condescending formula for expecting greater effort and energy from the non-ordained members of the church. Unless the church as a whole thinks theologically with far more rigour (and it is the episcopal traditions which need to do the more major re-appraisals) about the nature of all ministry, it will lose heart and purpose. All ministry derives from God before it derives from church. The ministry of the church, in whatever form, is the ministry of God in Christ, exercised through human beings. It follows therefore that all ministry is of equal value and equal dignity; in the context of eternity, there is no greater worth attaching to the ministry of any ordained ministry over and above the ministry of any other member of the Body of Christ. We all come from God and it is to God we return. It is from God that our ministry derives and it is to him that it will return. It is in baptism that God calls every member of the church to ministry, to a place and function within the continuing ministry of Christ on earth. Within the ministry of the whole church, the ministry of all the people of God, we believe that various specific functions have been given a specific seal – not a seal of approval so much as a seal of identity. But these ministries, ordained ministries, are not *superior* ministries because they have been identified, marked and authorised in the particular way we call ordination.

It is in this light that the whole church must reflect together on the ministry of women within the church. It may well be that within the Roman Catholic tradition the road to the ordination of women will not be opened in the very near future. Be that as it may, the matter surely becomes of very different significance if leadership is not located in the clergy alone. The entire Bible shows us powerful women in positions of authority, from Deborah in the Old Testament to those who were clearly in positions of leadership in the early church of whom (and to whom) Saint Paul writes. In the history of the Irish church, Saint Brigid – whoever and whatever she may have been – was certainly not a subordinate to anyone, least of all to any bishop! By vesting far too much authority and power in the hands of the ordained, the church has deprived itself of the God-given gifts and abilities of most of its members. This must surely border on being sin against the Holy Spirit. God has given us a totality of ministry within the totality of the membership of the church. God forbid – and surely God has forbidden – that the gifts of all the baptised, including the gifts of church leadership (whatever for ordained ministry), are to be found only within one gender and within one caste.

To return to the specificity of the ordained ministry, it must again be reiterated that the authority conveyed through ordination is located not in worldly power but in the doctrine of God. The ordained ministry focuses and represents specific aspects of the nature of the God who is within all ministry, whether ordained or non-ordained. With some admitted over-simplification,

I would seek to interpret the distinction of the ordained ministries within a context of the doctrine of God is this way: The bishop reflects the unity of God in representing the unity of Christian community, the priest the glory of God in administering the sacraments of the kingdom of God, and the deacon the compassion of God in serving those whom the world and the church have neglected and despised. It should follow that the bishop never ceases to be a priest and a deacon, and that the priest remains always a deacon. Christ's primary call to the disciples was, after all, to service, not to oversight. But every Christian disciple is also called to be a sign and instrument to the world of God's essential unity, glory and compassion. The difference is not that the ordained bishop, priest or deacon is necessarily better at this task, but that he or she is called sacramentallly to re-present – as well as to effect under God – this calling of God's grace within Christian community and in the world beyond it.

The crucial corollary is that the ministries of laity and clergy are therefore, in their essential nature, inter-dependent. As the fine American lay theologian, William Stringfellow, pointed out to an earlier generation, the clergy are called to serve the laity; the laity are called, with precisely the same authority, to serve the world. There can therefore be no authentic priesthood which is not a service to, and an enabling of, the ministry of God's people in the world. Too often, the clergy have accepted the role of being the face of the church to the world. And this has suited both clergy and laity. It has allowed the laity to regard the clergy as the paid presenters of religion both to them and to the world outside, and hence it has permitted them to become – as laity – the recipients of religion or (even more perilously) the hirers of religion for the world. Equally, the clergy have not shrunk from the prestige which, until recent times, went with being the public face of religion in Ireland. The theological truth must remain that the ministries of the ordained and non-ordained only have validity when they are, in their very essence, totally inter-dependent.

CHAPTER FIVE

By What Authority?

If there is ambivalence even within the Christian communities as to whether *authority* within the church – whether the authority of the bishop, priest, abbot, minister, pastor, synod, conference or council – is given by God or by the led community (and I would in fact suggest that there must always be an uneasy symbiosis between these two well-springs of authority), there is no such uncertainty among those who are not actively part of the church community.

There has developed in every part of public life – ecclesiastical and non-ecclesiastical alike – a far greater sense of leadership as ultimately dependent on its attractiveness to the led community. We see this in political life where few politicians will say things they know will be unpopular with the bulk of the electorate. Indeed a politician who wishes to rise in public esteem would seemingly do better in a communal crisis to 'feel the pain' of those around (and as mawkishly as is possible) than to deliver any form of rigorous or reflective leadership which does not link in with the public mood. We certainly see that the predictable temptation has arisen for those in ecclesiastical authority to seek public popularity and to catch the public mood with a new fervour. Some years ago, preaching at the consecration of a new bishop, I pointed out that he need not regard himself as a politician in need of re-election. He was being given freedom to lead, rather than an obligation to 'nurse his constituency'. Bishops, perhaps particularly within the Church of Ireland tradition, have long been accused of lacking backbone, and of pandering to the more truculent and vociferous of their flocks. It is a dangerous situation when bishops, clergy or others involved in the leadership of the church are more concerned with being liked, than with being trusted as principled (even if sometimes wrongheaded). And there can be little doubt that church leaders in a post-Catholic populist culture must guard ever more carefully against being 'all things to all people', in order to protect a specious authority which is in practice little more than an echo chamber for popular sentiment.

But as the religious landmarks of the past are seen to have less intrinsic authority, and as unbridled individualism becomes ever more a feature of Irish society, consumerism in religion, as in all else, is the obvious consequence. The controlling feature for membership of a Christian tradition becomes its desirability for the individual. The question, 'Does what the church is saying suit me?', now seems a perfectly legitimate enquiry for the church-goer to make. It may be argued that the cult of the individual has been around for a very long time, but what is certain is that it has unquestionably taken on new momentum in an Ireland where community is fragmenting with immense speed.

Any espousal of *hierarchical authority* is therefore as politically incorrect as it is possible to be in the culture of Ireland today. Any authority which is not severely circumscribed by accountability appears dangerous enough, but *hierarchy* seems a great deal worse. The latter term seems redolent of limitless power, non-accountability, non-transparency, and – potentially at least – all the abuses associated with non-elected rule. Ecclesiastical hierarchy in particular seems to equate with subjugation of others and the suppression of freedom and pleasure. Nor is this anything new. From Reformation times, there have been many who believed that bishops were emphatically not in the best interests of the church.

Whatever for bishops, it is in fact a fallacy to assume that more than a very few communities of any kind – ecclesiastical or not – have ever been other than hierarchical, even if the terminology of hierarchy was avoided. Post-Enlightenment Europe, for all its public espousal of democracy, has not produced many totally egalitarian communities. Hierarchy in society implies some ranking or pecking order, and for the ranking to be based on economic rather than more traditional factors does not make it less of a hierarchy. There is a hierarchy in western society today. Money and economic power control society (and increasingly so in an increasingly globalised economy), but their hierarchs are no less part of a hierarchy because they are not termed as such. Traditionally, however, the term is used where the assumption is made that the legitimacy of the hierarchy's authority to rule is rooted in a reference point beyond itself. In the case of the church, this point of reference for the authority of hierarchy is usually taken to be the rule of God.

Historically, however, the church for more than half of its existence was little different from surrounding society in this respect. Until early modern times, society was explicitly hierarchical. The notion of the divine right of kings may not seem very pertinent today, but it was almost universally accepted through most of the period of Christendom. And it was not only kings whose place in society was seen as ultimately God-given. Rulers and lords, great or small, were believed to have been placed in their positions in society by God. There was no notion that the authority to rule was a reward to an individual for good behaviour or great abilities, but rather it was believed that this state of affairs had been ordered by God, and was therefore immutable. Authority to rule was not earned, nor were rulers answerable to those they ruled; authority was given by a transcendent God and it was to God that rulers were finally accountable for their stewardship of power. This did not mean that there were not continuing attempts right through recorded history to remove rulers, either by ambitious pretenders, by invading armies, or by disaffected subjects. But the basis of human authority was not located in democratic consent. In principle if not always in practice, the pre-modern world would have argued that all authority came from God, from a transcendent force and final authority.

The post-Enlightenment world – the world of modernism – has given less and less space to the transcendent or to God. In the post-modern world, the transcendent has become an exclusively subjective perception. The transcendent is most likely to be that which makes the individual feel good or somehow more elated or elevated than usual. The transcendent may be an aesthetic experience, or merely the warm glow of good companions. It certainly has no objective status or reality. Modernism and post-modernism (and there is perhaps less distinction between the two than is at times asserted) are part of the maelstrom of post-Catholic Ireland. They have undeniably had a considerable effect on the psyche of the Irish culture as we now experience it. It is neither the transcendent nor God but humankind, in the eyes of our culture, which is becoming the reference point for all reality and hence for authority, if there is to be any. Within such a prevailing mind-set, the Christian Church appears to many of its adherents – not to mention those who are not within its ambit – as a human institution rather than a God-given community of grace. In other words, one does not need to be a non-believer in today's world to make an assumption that the church was founded by good and well-meaning people, rather than provided by God. Belonging to church has become a matter of consumer choice rather than spiritual necessity.

For those who look in upon the church from outside, the church cannot justifiably claim to have any rights which are not validated by, or subject to, the 'real world' outside. The church must be subject, or at any rate amenable, to the rule of state law. In the Ireland of recent times, this has indeed become a serious issue. The Constitution of Ireland allows church communities to order their own affairs without interference from the state. But where there is a conflict between the law of the state and the law of any particular Christian tradition (and naturally and in particular, where the criminal law of the state is involved), then increasingly the balance is moving towards the priority of the law of the land. The internal constitution or canon law of any ecclesial community has now very little more *a priori* authority than the rules of a sports club. A sports club may have its own internal regulations but, where these seem to violate the principles of natural justice, the law of the state is free to intervene and, where the criminal law has been breached, the state must intervene. If the Irish state is still a little squeamish about reducing the internal laws of any church community to the status of the rules of a club, the courts of Strasbourg are already beginning to demonstrate that they will have no such qualms.

In a culture which believes itself (albeit not entirely justifiably) to be fully democratised, and that within civilised society all authority is conditional on its popularity with those 'under authority', the authority structures of the church are ever more under scrutiny, as much by those inside the church as by those outside. An undertaking of categorical obedience – whether to a bishop, a conference, or an abbot – seems anachronistic in a world which has individualised the person to such a degree that community itself has come to be judged by its usefulness to the given individual rather than as a necessary basis for responsible living.

The only reasonable response by the church is to make certain that its 'rules' are coherent and convincing rather than merely the fruits of its intrinsic authority. It was, I think, Leonardo da Vinci who once said that anyone who uses authority as the defining issue in any argument is using not wisdom but merely memory. Many years ago, a senior military officer – speaking to a group of junior clergy of which I was part – defined the gift of leadership as the ability to make sense of the rules to everyone concerned. This means two things. First, that if the rules are in fact only human conventions and no longer meet the exigencies of the situation, they may indeed be seen as requiring modification or removal. If, on the other hand, a particular rule is intrinsic to the entire philosophy of the body concerned, then this must be explained and justified. The freedom offered by Christ for individuals to grow into the stature of their personhood which God has willed for them cannot be metamorphosed by the institution of the church into a religious rule book.

None of the Christian traditions has been spectacularly successful in achieving a balanced approach to a leadership which maintains an authority by making sense of the rules. The notion that 'rules are rules are rules' comes more readily to mind. Discerning which of the church's rules are human conventions or conveniences (albeit sensible and even godly in some human contexts) and which are of the essence of the Christian gospel is of course no simple task. It requires spiritual humility in addition to an equally spiritual wisdom to make such judgements. And it certainly demands the involvement of a wider grouping than merely the ordained.

In many of our Christian traditions in Ireland, ecclesial authority is not vested in the few, but is more widely dispersed. Anglicanism on the world stage is at present certainly no example of a working church polity, but its structures for church government within provinces may sometimes display useful features. In Ireland, Anglicanism attempts to balance an episcopal tradition with a synodical government that involves clergy and laity in addition to the bishops. For the most part this works moderately well in a slightly shambling way, and has the strength that it does give a genuine place both to the episcopal tradition and to a precept of *consensus fidelium* which is more than theoretical. Tensions inevitably arise when the question is asked as to who does in fact have 'the final say' for the church? Is it to be the bishops collectively, or is the General Synod of the church? The typically dissembling Anglican answer is that it is both! The bishops cannot impose legislation on the Church of Ireland. Nor can the General Synod make any alteration to the doctrines of the church against the will of the bishops. When it comes to making decisions on matters to do with the moral teaching of the church – as moral norms and ethical perspectives change within society (and as these are, sometimes misguidedly, perceived as being of doctrinal import) – the situation may well become more fraught in future years.

The purpose of what has just been written was not to laud one Christian tradition for its particular *modus operandi* (which is at times akin to an almost total paralysis), but merely to suggest that there are possibilities in attempting to balance the inherited traditions of the whole Catholic Church with an attentiveness to the God-given responsibilities of the whole people of God, in order that the wholeness and wholesomeness of the church may be furthered. We are left with the question of whether a dispersed authority – as it is sometimes termed – is a genuine authority at all. Can the interpretation of Christian doctrine be decided by majority decision within a large synodical grouping, many of whose members may have little theological competence? What then constitutes 'expert opinion', when it comes to the clarification of theological matters? Is it to be a pope or a patriarch on individual authority? Is it to be bishops alone as guardians of the faith (or, *mutatis mutandis*, a council of ordained church leaders in the more Protestant traditions)? Or is it to be bishops and clergy in convocation, or some equivalent? Or is it to be bishops, clergy and people in synod? Or is it to be decided with the guidance of professional theologians who will almost certainly have greater scholarly understanding of the issues involved than any or all of the groupings mentioned above? This flurry of largely rhetorical questions may elicit no immediate answer. What they may suggest is that there must be a reasonable and mutually respectful balance between the different constituent parts of the Body of Christ, if the church is to be fully what it is called by God to be. The challenge is to ensure that a perfect balance does not impose total immobility.

From any consideration of the nature of authority within the church, we are drawn ineluctably to a more practical issue as to whether tenure to any specific post within the church should be permanent or not. Society has become used to the idea that leadership is never given for an open-ended period of time. Within the Protestant traditions, there has been a long tradition whereby those holding the presidential or moderatorial office do so for a very limited time. At congregational level, a Methodist minister's appointment of office as pastor will be little over six or seven years. And within the Roman Catholic and Anglican religious orders also, posts of authority are not held for life. There are clearly opportunities and challenges inherent in such a model. Leaving aside the question as to whether one is ordained 'for ever', whether as bishop, priest or minister, there remains the totally different matter as to whether the good of the church might be better served if the holding of any particular post were to be for a specified period only.

One certain advantage is, to put it crudely, that long-term damage is less likely to be done if no individual may remain in any ecclesiastical post for a long period. The concomitant disadvantage is that placing time constraints around a particular task may in fact prevent great good from being done. It is sometimes commented that if, for example, a position in a church is to be held for five years, the first and last years are spent respectively in settling in, and in preparing to leave; any good work is done for a period of three years. There is also the danger that politicisation of roles of ministerial leadership becomes an ever greater threat if these are held as short-term appointments. In the Irish legal system, there is the eminently sensible conviction – if we were to draw a less than complete parallel – that it is safer that those appointed to the judiciary of the country do not stand for re-election every few years. Perhaps we may be satisfied with a conviction that if personal status and cachet is removed from any role within the church, and if all ministry is exercised in genuine collaboration with the entire Christian community, matters as to the advisability of fixed-term appointments assume different proportions. It should most certainly be made possible for a man or woman to move from any ministry within the church to any other ministry without a loss, whether real or perceived, of human worth or dignity.

The church, for all that its business is to do with the transcendent, cannot expect that it will remain uninfluenced by the perception of society that all authority – ecclesial or otherwise – draws its validation only from the consent and the satisfaction of the community. Yet the church cannot negotiate away that which is fundamental to its very existence, obedience to Christ rather than the world. It may however learn – through its exposure to a new, draughtier and less friendly world around it – that while its obedience must be always and only to Christ, the realities of the transcendent to the visible and tangible world will be better mediated by the whole people of God than by individual or hierarchical *fiat* of power. There can be no authority for the church as whole without leadership. This authority and leadership may now have to become a less than tidy thing, but then the grace of God has never been known for its intrinsic tidiness either.

CHAPTER SIX

Hope for Ideology

In the political and social culture of today's Ireland, it is probably less perilous to deny any ideological motivation for anything, than to admit to enthusiasm. Indeed, the entire socio-political scene in Ireland appears at times to be almost devoid of any robust ideological standpoint. For many people, ideas and ideals – whether those of religion or of a non-religious ideology – appear as uniformly perfidious. The French playright Eugène Ionesco could thus classify religion and ideology together in this respect, and find them equivalently repugnant and dangerous, suggesting that whereas in the name of religion, one tortures, persecutes, and builds pyres, it is in the guise of ideologies that one actually massacres, tortures and kills. Given that Ireland is now emerging from a prolonged period of political violence which has had religious as well as political overtones, it may not be entirely surprising that many people today wish simply to get on with the business of living without recourse to any form of ideology or idealism. But yet we need to think of the background, not merely to the Ireland, but to the *Europe* in which we live.

The European project itself was built on an ideology. Following the Second World War, there was the genuine belief that active structured co-operation between European countries would destroy the instincts that had made for such destructive war between the nations of the continent twice in little more than a single generation. Much has been achieved but, writing as a genuine and enthusiastic Europhile, I cannot but feel some deep anxieties. For all that Jacques Delors pleaded for a soul for Europe, the structures of the European Union are seemingly becoming utterly unconcerned for any value systems that cannot be homogenised for the entire Union. It is undeniably true that human rights feature high on European agendas but invariably within the context of the rights of individuals, rather than the responsibilities of either individuals or communities to community itself. The concern for an almost totalitarian homogenisation is well-meant, but it emerges into practice as deeply one-dimensional and truly soul-less.

The expansion of Europe has been in many respects altruistic. But one is left with an uncomfortable feeling that it contains within it seeds of an even greater thrust towards a standardisation of the externals of law and 'practice', but without much awareness of the need for community heart, or for any ideology that sees the common good in three-dimensional terms. The debate on a constitution for Europe has involved different Christian traditions in considering whether or not the name of God should be used and, indeed, whether reference should be made to the Christian heritage of Europe. It is surely more important that the reality of God is apparent in Europe, and that the Christian heritage appears as of more than archaeological or cultural interest. The church exists, in part at least, to preserve that which in its past has enabled men and women to live with wisdom, and retains the power to do so in the future. There is no doubt that much of what the Europe of today now is derives from its development through the centuries of Christendom. And the alternative to a coherent religious sound in Europe may well be a descent into a wasteland of bureaucratic banality. And Hannah Arendt's often-quoted aphorism concerning the sheer banality of evil means that it is probably easier to move from a soulless homogenisation through the gates of totalitarianism than we would wish to believe. Religion does not free any nation or community from the dangers of tyranny and of repression. Indeed many dictatorships have been established with the complicity and support of religion. Nevertheless, the absence of any ideology in support of a common good is certainly no safeguard against a descent into cruelty and despotism.

What has become true of Europe as a whole is apparent also

within the Ireland of a post-Catholic culture. 'Independent Ireland', for almost the entire twentieth century, was built on an ideological narrative, an ideology founded on a particular mythology (using 'mythology' in the sense of the story with the power to change people, as distinct from mythology as untruth). The story of independent Ireland was constructed on the mythology of an Ireland which had been tyrannised for centuries by its nearest neighbour and which had been delivered from this repression by heroic figures, in particular the leaders of the 1916 Rising. This mythology was given an almost spiritual status, and ultimately this quasi-religious ideology was not open for questioning. It was not a particularly wholesome ideology, but it was the cultural framework which shaped the Ireland that has existed until the past decade. It was also – as I suggested in an earlier chapter – linked to a religious identity, particularly in relation to the Catholic Church.

In current jargon, it was the meta-narrative, the great story which made sense of everything. It was a fundamental ideology from which other ideologies could emerge. And good ideologies could and did emerge. A sense of responsibility for the weaker in society, the belief that there was such a thing as community for which individuals had responsibility, and even a degree of awareness of communal accountability to the Ireland we had been given by the sacrifice of others – all of these instincts were there to be seen, and they derived (to some degree at least) as much from the fundamental Irish meta-narrative, as much as from inherited religious faith. But the meta-narrative of modern Ireland has gone for ever, as both a societal sense of history and an inhering place for the church in present-day Irish society have been consigned to the refuse heap in post-modern nowness. It has not been replaced by any new ideology, wholesome or unwholesome.

The political life of Ireland now appears increasingly to revolve around short-term expediency, and the need to gain power or to retain power. For a government to offend the powerful of this country or any other country on a point of ideological principle is never going to be given the public respect and support it surely deserves. When Shannon Airport was kept available for the use of American military planes during the second Iraqi invasion of 2003, the alternative was to risk losing the goodwill and favour of the United States, with the possible consequence of reprisals, with the removal of financial investment from a country which had benefited so enormously from such investment. It is however totally pointless to blame one particular government for the politics of pragmatism and the death of ideology. Ideology, as I have suggested, is for the most part regarded as a dangerous distraction within a culture which has tended consciously to eschew a sense of history and the transcendental alike.

It is very easy to blame the phenomenon of post-modernism for everything we do not like in our present-day culture, but this would be far too superficial as a single explanation. It is undoubtedly true that the philosophy of life in the western world stresses individualism rather than community, and often sees truth itself as something which is personal and transitory rather than objective and fixed. But this is only part of the picture. Modernism remains as very much established within the psyche of people and communities. This is the mindset which attaches complete significance only to that which can be empirically verified or is scientifically demonstrable. There is a viewpoint which would argue that post-modernism is actually less inimical to religion than was modernism. Religion does not have to apologise for itself in a world which is unconcerned with the objectively verifiable, and which does not challenge any form of individual and individualistic exploration into the meaning of existence. But this cannot be the end of the matter. The Christian religion does base itself on certain non-negotiables. There may be much dispute and even conflict when it comes to the precise articulation of these non-negotiables, but Christianity is a faith which takes history, the events of history, and God's action through human history as of supreme importance. All ideology, whether religious, political or social, requires some non-negotiables.

If we accept that the cultural mindset on the cusp of modernism and of a post-modernism (which latter we do not yet fully understand) is a contributory factor in the decline of any ideology, we may also assume that the remarkable improvement in the material conditions in which many Irish people live is also a factor. Ireland's residents now have one of the highest average *per capita* incomes in the world. Personal comfort is no stimulus to an ideological outlook. The certainty that the relatively high income of many people has been achieved at a price of over-work and dislocation from the community either of birth (or even of current residence) has deprived people of the space that is necessary for coherent thought or any deep consideration of what life might essentially be for. A hunger for a communal social justice or for compassionate generosity, within either the individual or community soul, has now neither the room nor the time in which to develop.

We are faced with the scandal that Ireland is also a country deeply divided between those who have plenty, and those who have insufficient material means for any secure existence. For all that the country as a whole is now wealthier than it has ever been in the past, poverty and homelessness have not been eradicated. In contrast to many of our political partners in Europe, Ireland spends very little on public services. Indeed some of our European neighbours spend almost twice as high a proportion of Gross National Product (GNP) on their public services than does Ireland. To spend more in order to ensure that health or education services were equally available to all – regardless of income – would require higher rates of income tax. Sadly, this is a nettle which major political parties seem unwilling to advocate in forthright terms. In a country where there is little ideological concern for the homeless or the deprived, there will be few votes for any who threaten to reduce the income of the comfortably off.

On the larger canvas, the ideological impulse, certainly on a political level, has been weakened with the fall of communism in Europe. We might certainly argue that this has been a price worth paying. Communism brought untold misery to millions of people. It was a ruthless totalitarian system with very little to commend it. Although all this is certainly true, it is also tragic that there is today no alternative ideology to interrogate and challenge the injustices which are part of an untrammelled and *laissez-faire* capitalism which now holds sway in the developed world. Marxism may indeed have been defective as a political philosophy, but its central theses are proving compelling in the world of today. Marxism preached that economic greed is the factor to be found behind all political change and development, and that those who have power and possessions will – unless compelled to behave otherwise – oppress those who cannot oppose them. With the fall of communist regimes has come the discrediting of an ideology which, for all its flaws, argued that social justice was not something that just happened because people were intrinsically good or naturally kind.

Since partition, Ireland has never known the politics of left and right to any great degree. In Northern Ireland, the political divides were those of unionism and nationalism. In the Free State and later the Republic, the divisions were grounded more in the politics of the Civil War of the early 1920s than in a great deal that was more recent. It is true that the Irish Labour movement had proud origins in the early years of the twentieth century but few could suggest that the Labour Party was ever a particularly potent force within the political life of Ireland. When the party formed part of a coalition government, it could only ever be as a junior partner to one of the established parties which were not, of their nature, left of centre. The decline of interest in old-fashioned nationalism in southern Ireland (and certainly in the politics of a civil war which had taken place eighty years earlier) has left a serious vacuum in political definition. In the society of Ireland today, which – because some advances have been made in the provision of education – fondly believes that it is egalitarian and has even become a meritocracy, there is little place in its heart for those who are seen as the losers. What is in effect moral blame has come to be attached to those who have not been successful in life. It has sometimes been said that one

HOPE FOR IDEOLOGY

may judge a church by how it handles its failures. The same may reasonably be said of any society. One may surely judge any society by how it deals with those within it who are powerless whether because of poverty, illness, or old age.

And so it appears as though there is a singular reluctance among the main political parties to present any coherent ideological standpoint at present. This would, no doubt, be denied by their party officials or political representatives. But voters in national elections – and in fact fewer and fewer people seem to regard it as worth their while to vote, which is in itself saying something profound – cannot truly be certain as to what difference a vote for any mainstream party would mean. Democracy is a fragile plant. It requires not only the consent of a population but also shared values of mutual respect, the rule of law and the furthering of the rights of its minorities as much as of its majorities. If it is to flourish it therefore requires the involvement of ideologues and idealists. The task of politics in a democracy must have elements of a vocation. Politics should draw men and women who could achieve in other walks of life but who nevertheless choose politics as a noble calling. Otherwise democracy slides into populism.

It is true that no politician can afford to be hated by the electorate, but an entirely populist politician has no policy other than to be popular and hence to be elected to office. The purpose of being in power can become little more than precisely that single ambition, to be in power. Democracy has then very little to do with what is sometimes glibly called the common good, and a great deal more to do with a series of public performances by members of the political class who will not offer genuine ideological alternatives. This is a treacherous path which endangers democracy itself. Not 'doing the vision thing' may work well as a short term expedient for the politician in the hunt for votes. But if democratic politicians will not dream dreams, and seek to transfer their ideals into realities, there are others on the edges who will take their place. Those who are not constrained by the tenets of democracy only require the maltreatment of democracy in order to open their path to the subversion of the entire democratic process.

It might be argued that the only ideological (or cogent) analysis on social issues in Ireland which lucidly and compellingly challenges the principal political parties comes from within the Roman Catholic Church – the Conference of Religious of Ireland, CORI. Here one encounters compelling, reasoned and well-researched analyses of the social state of the country. It is one of the terrible by-products of the damage done to the reputation of the church that CORI's witness to justice and righteousness may safely be sidelined by those in power. And CORI is, in any case, an exception in the life of the Christian Church in Ireland. There are of course individuals and smaller communities within all the Christian traditions whose witness and work for social concern is well-attested. But the church, *qua* church, is still finding it difficult to present any coherent ideological standpoint on the nature of society and community. Reasons may be found in the lack of confidence the church has in its own public *persona*. But the lack of an ideological mindset within the church surely requires further explanation than the nervousness of an institution which has lost public credibility. This may lie in the reality that the spirit of populism, so evident in public life, has also infected the church. Popularity is a dangerous chimera in any Christian community. Ideologues are rarely concerned if they are popular. They are more concerned that they are getting a principled message through to those who should hear, a characteristic which the leaders of Christian communities would do well to consider. We will never hear the compelling whisper of God if the ideological spirit is banished. The absence of idology is not silence, it is a cacophony of conflicting screams.

We are left with the challenge as to how the church itself can recover a spirit of vibrant ideology. Ideology is at the heart of the message of Christianity. Christianity is, after all, about sanctification, about a call to holiness. The entire Judeo-Christian tradition speaks about the need for believers to challenge the evils that are systemic within the structures of society. More to the point, perhaps, is the famous injunction of the writer of the Proverbs of the Hebrew Bible (Proverbs 29:18), 'Where there is no vision the people perish'. A better translation would suggest that without prophetic leadership, people will lose all restraint, an even more sobering thought. One cannot have a Christian faith which is not profoundly ideological, and yet the ideological spirit is little visible within the mainstream Christian traditions of Ireland today.

Christianity can be built on one ideology – love alone: the radiant love of God for his creation in its entirety, a love which is to be reflected in everything that the church is and does, both corporately and through the lives of individual disciples. Love has been given an entirely human framework in our society, although this is nothing new. We return again to Herbert for perceptive insight into the way in which the love of God has been humanised and hence dehumanised:

Immortal Love, author of this great frame,
Sprung from the beauty which can never fade;
How hath man parcel'd out thy glorious name,
And thrown it on that dust which thou hast made,
While mortal love doth all that title gain!
Which siding with invention, they together
Bear all the sway, possessing heart and brain,
(Thy workmanship) and give thee share in neither.[8]

The only ideology on which the church can stand is that which restores love to its origins in the heart of God. Only thus can a human love of heart and brain be given its true perspective and unleashed for a genuine creativity. Yet survival rather than any ideology of divine love seems to be the keyword for our sad institutional church. And yet, as Christians must remind themselves constantly, the quest for survival can never be the Christian priority, nor is it of the essence of love, human or divine.

In social terms, the church must unitedly apply its ideology, and support those (of any faith and none) who challenge a sys-

---

8. George Herbert, 'Love I', op. cit., p 51.

temic selfishness of society, an inculturated self-indulgence which allows huge extremes of wealth and poverty to continue in a country which has enough wealth for all its citizens, were that wealth to be more evenly divided. Taking such a stance will inevitably lead to confrontation within the church, which has among its membership many who are more than content with the present social and economic structures of the country. But to neglect this challenge, in fear of material consequences for the church, is to ignore the basic ideology on which the gospel is built, the love of God for all his creation in a complete impartiality and equality.

Only when the righteous can find the courage to question and confront the absence of truly ideological stances in the political life of the country can the Christian community ever hope to be taken seriously by anyone. But to be taken seriously it must first demonstrate that it is itself fuelled by an ideology, the belief that humanity is called under God to individual and communal righteousness, a righteousness which is not content with the salvation of the individual soul alone, but with the creation of a community where love, justice and truth are to flourish.

CHAPTER SEVEN

Coping with Culture – Niebuhr Revisited

If the Irish church is to communicate a clear ideology in word and action – the unconditional love of God for his creation and the call of God to his people to reflect that unconditional love in their dealings with the whole of creation – advantage will certainly be taken of it. This need not be surprising. After all if any life on earth was taken advantage of, it was that of Christ himself. There can be few clergy (and even fewer faithful clergy) who have never been hoodwinked by the clever conman. In most cases, the cause is an entirely honourable anxiety that this particular request – implausible and far-fetched as it may seem – might in fact be utterly genuine. There is no shame attached to this. A lack of concern is a greater defect of character than any naïve gullibility. What may happen, in terms of duping, to the individual pastor may happen also to the institutional church. Perhaps at times it should happen. But the church must nevertheless have a clarity about its relationship to the world around it. If it is ever to regain the trust of the Irish people, it must show that its love is unconditional and not a masquerade for the regaining of control. The church must never again seek the craven obedience of the Irish people; such obedience will in any case never again be forthcoming. But the church must nevertheless seek to develop a new relationship to the culture in which it is set.

Although it is now over fifty years since Richard Niebuhr delivered a series of lectures in Texas which were later to become the classic text, *Christ and Culture*, his analysis (although not without its flaws and even less without its critics) remains persuasive and valuable for our generation. Setting *Christ* and *Culture* as distinct entities or poles, Niebuhr advanced a set of possible relationships between them, none of which he promoted as ultimately appropriate nor belittled as totally amiss. These relationships were 'Christ against Culture', 'Christ of Culture', 'Christ above Culture', 'Christ and Culture in Paradox', and 'Christ transforming Culture'. The titles are for the most part self-explanatory, but two initial observations might be made. The first is that there are elements of all of these to be found in biblical teaching. The second is that, although Niebuhr used the terminology of 'Christ and Culture', much of what he had to say may readily be understood in terms of 'Church and Culture'. The church in Ireland may well find that it is forced, in obedience to the gospel, to promote differing interactions with the prevailing Irish culture in different circumstances, but it needs to find clarity of understanding if it is not to fall slavishly into shallow conformity to the culture or an equally shallow separatism from that culture. I am grateful to a number of commentators for their elucidations of Niebuhr's writing in what now follows.

The first of Niebuhr's group, *Christ against Culture*, is the separatist inclination. The church of post-Catholic Ireland may indeed wish to set itself implacably against the way in which Ireland is moving and changing and, as further secularisation looms, encourage its own membership to a holy separateness from society, the posture of an open repudiation of surrounding mores and societal changes. There are, however, inherent contradictions within this standpoint. By withdrawing from surrounding culture – and this is in fact impossible, as our language and thought patterns are all highly influenced by the culture in which we live – we are merely creating a different culture, and one which is as fallible and as open to sin as the culture we believe we have rejected. To oppose the surrounding culture *per se* is also a misunderstanding of what holiness is, and more seriously it is seeing sin as something which is not systemic in any and every community.

By definition, the incarnate Christ cannot have been somehow outside the culture of first century Palestine; if he were to have been, his humanity was a sham. To be human is to be within a particular culture. There are certainly moments when the church must be ready to challenge the surrounding culture in the name of Christ, but this cannot be its habitual disposition.

The model of the *Christ of Culture*, on the other hand, sees no cause for conflict between Christ and the surrounding culture. In this understanding, Christ is the highest fulfilment of all culture. Thus, he is to be found within every culture which may, in all aspects, be seen thereby as interrelated with Christ. There is an underlying accommodationism here that certainly blunts the cutting edge of the gospel, and would tend to reconcile Christianity with anything that culture happens to regard as acceptable. Yet, having accepted this *caveat*, we need also to recognise that Christians must at all times be attentive to what is happening around them if they are to understand the totality of Christianity itself more fully. There are times when God's Word is revealed through societal change. To give one rather obvious example, the death penalty is today regarded as unacceptable by all governments in the European Union to the degree that no country retaining the death penalty may become part of the Union, but in western Europe it was not the church which led the case against the death penalty. Yet the European church for the most part nevertheless accepts today that the death penalty – although perfectly acceptable within the pages of scripture – can no longer sit comfortably with Christianity. There are times when there is an unfolding through human history of fuller implications of the scriptures which are not immediately evident from the text of the Bible itself. Thus, slavery might be regarded – from the pages of scripture – as socially acceptable, but within the past two centuries, it has become apparent that slavery is not consistent with the most basic implications of the gospel. There are times and places when the prevailing culture can teach Christianity to look more deeply at the message of Christianity. There are also times when finding Christ in a cultural development is blasphemous. A wise old English cleric, Dean Inge, did once warn that the church which married the spirit of the present age would be a widower in the next. The dilemma is that the church might simply keep re-marrying.

There is another aspect to the acceptance that the vision of a *Christ of Culture* is not entirely misguided. If Christianity cannot be translated into the grammar of any culture, it is not an incarnational faith. When they travelled to convert the world, Christian missionaries over many generations carried, preached, and sought to impose, not only the faith but an entire western way of life. This was probably not seen as patent imperialism but, because the Christian faith and the culture from which they themselves had originated seemed as of one piece in the minds and hearts of the missionaries, faith and culture were proclaimed as a single entity. The inevitable if unforseeable consequence was that the rejection of western culture readily became a rejection of Christianity itself. If Christianity cannot be interpreted and understood in the language and culture of any community, it is inadequate for its task. In that sense, Christ must indeed be within the culture of anywhere and everywhere. The Word of God cannot be excluded from anywhere.

The paradigm of a *Christ above Culture* fits perfectly with the Christian tradition known as 'natural law'. This view of God and creation sees within the natural order in all its aspects the hand of God, the God of creation. Therefore, there is much within the natural order which is God-given and God-inspired even if it is not restricted or specific to the Christian viewpoint. The God of the Christian faith is the culmination of nature. It is thus the task of the church to lead people above and beyond a culture which cannot of itself be wholly corrupt, because it is founded on what God gave to the world in nature and – as one of the creation narratives in Genesis puts it – God saw what he had made 'and it was very good'. This attitude to surrounding culture, almost as part of the route to Christian perfection, has a vast amount to teach the Irish church of today. It gives the incarnation real meaning. It refuses to suggest that the Word of God may be banished from any part of the created order. If it has any inherent weaknesses, it is in its predisposition to regard nature as static, and human inventiveness as suspect. It is also predicated on a relationship between church and world which is intrinsically stable and entwined.

Christ and Culture in paradox differs from the notion of the Christ who is above culture in that it fully recognises that there is an inevitable tension between Christ and culture which will not be resolved. This is based on a theology which envisions two domains of reality – the realm of grace and the realm of law – and is most characteristic of the Lutheran tradition within the church. There is a continuing tension between the two domains. The Christian, being inherently sinful, must live in the realm of grace, but Luther himself never believed that the realm of law, represented by the state, could thereby be swept aside. A Christian is subject to temporal law and must obey that law even if this, of itself, does not remove the state of sin in which all humans are submerged and which requires the operation of God's grace for personal redemption. The viewpoint of *Christ and Culture in paradox* has the advantage that it rejects a simplistic separatism or pietism. The Christian must live in the realms both of grace and of law, even if it is grace which will ultimately redeem the individual. But there is much here which leads, rather like the *Christ above Culture* paradigm, to a cultural conservatism and stagnation. As the Lutherans of the 'Confessing Church' learnt amidst the horrors of Nazi Germany, there are times and places when there must be higher judgement – the judgement of Christ – on the recognised law of the state, and a conscientious rejection of that law by Christians as demonic rather than of God.

The last of Niebuhr's paradigms, *Christ transforming Culture*, is (on the surface at least) the most compelling. This is the call to overcome culture and to create a culture of holiness. Niebuhr is careful to suggest that this cannot be done by strenuous effort alone. If a culture is transformed by Christianity, this is a work of God's grace. It is indeed difficult to find many examples of where a church-driven transformation of culture produced lasting good, and it must be noted that any genuine theocracy – a supposed 'rule of the state by God' – has almost inevitably toppled over into totalitarianism, usually of a particularly noxious kind. On the other hand, the conviction that the church can and must influence the surrounding culture is something which must surely remain at the forefront of the Christian engagement with society.

As Niebuhr made very clear, none of his models for Christian engagement with culture should be regarded as totally flawed, and nor should any of them to be seen as the only proper course for the mission of the church. Each model of praxis could claim an authenticity from within both the scriptures and the history of the Christian tradition, and each has inherent difficulties. But what is of most importance to the Irish church of today is that it finds a process through which it may carefully and unitedly decide on which particular attitude to the surrounding culture is the most appropriate for differing situations.

For some years, I have been suggesting that the time is ripe for a 'Synod of the Irish church', the whole Irish church. Such a synod should include leadership from the different mainstream Christian traditions, should involve ordained and non-ordained, drawing from local and central experience, and should obviously include both men and women. An exploration of the church's relationship with the culture of today's Ireland might make the most appropriate starting point for an agenda, for it is more than certain that if the Irish church does not face Ireland as the united face of Christian witness, post-Catholic Ireland will not listen to it. The church must be ready to proposition Ireland and to engage with the realities of Irish culture today, but this it will never be able to do as a series of competing religious brands and logos.

CHAPTER EIGHT

Growing Unity

Although a major ecclesiastical and even academic industry, ecumenism has also become an ecclesiastical cliché (if perhaps slightly less an academic cliché). Greater unity between Christian traditions is ultimately something which is to be done rather than talked about. And, despite the ominous sense of 'two paces forward and one pace back' which seems to pervade the international ecumenical scene at present, there are always real hopes for growing a unity between Christian traditions. This is surely the insistent urging of God, despite the barriers of arrogance and complacency that human institutions persist on placing before attempts to find a greater harmony and unity of purpose within Christ's household of faith.

Too often, the question being asked is the wrong one. The traditions of the church become more fixated on the matters that divide them, and the question posed – even subliminally – is, 'How much divergence can we accept, before Christian brothers and sisters are permitted to recognise, and witness to, an essential unity before a secondary disunity?' The better question must surely be, 'How much do the different traditions need to hold in common, before they can place the central shared truths of the call of Christ before all else?' This is not a formula for any instant, visible and organic unity. It may perhaps be a nudge towards a change in mindset which the church so desperately needs.

Shortly after the Second World War, the World Council of Churches proposed what became know as the Lund principle. The Lund principle is that the different Christian communities should set themselves to do nothing apart that they can, in conscience, do together. Only good reasons – including of course serious reasons of conscience – should justify different church communities in any situation working as separate bodies. It is a principle which the different Christian traditions have almost totally ignored. Many excuses have been given, but the primary reason may only be that each tradition fears the loss of its own identity if it were to co-operate too freely with other traditions. The irony is that even small signs of minimal co-operation between different denominations would indicate to a disenchanted world that Christians do in fact believe that the gospel is more important than the autonomy of their own particular fiefdoms. At this stage in the history of Irish Christianity, the different Christian traditions should be sharing churches, even if worship is not always shared. It need acarcely be added that worship should of course be shared a great deal more than it is. If the sharing in the eucharist is to continue to be a matter of difficulty for some traditions, surely a sharing of the Word of God between Christians of different traditions cannot present too many problems, even to the most fastidious. The description of the early Christian Church in the Acts of the Apostles makes it abundantly clear that a great deal more was shared than the sacraments. They shared prayer and the scriptures, and they shared belongings.

Very few of the mainstream Christian traditions have sufficient resources for their needs. Some of the reformed traditions in the southern part of the island have very scattered flocks. We are still at a stage of self-delusion where the absurdity of a refusal to share not only resources but also pastoral care in a structured way has barely dawned on those in authority. Informally, there is frequently a tremendous pastoral care taken of people of minority traditions who are isolated from others of their own denomination, by local clergy and neighbours. But there is still not the courage to make this pastoral care something which both traditions may formally recognise and approve. In the majority Catholic tradition, there is a real shortage of clergy in some parishes. Parishes which might have had three or four curates in the recent past are now in the care of one priest, perhaps in old age. Why should some of the immense pastoral work-load not be shared with clergy of other traditions? In both the situations outlined here, there is on all sides the unspoken fear of offending the more conservative of the laity, but also the sneaking suspicion that people might be seduced away to another tradition if the pastoral care given by that tradition was particularly effective and caring. Behind all of this caution is a terrible cancerous fear – fear of people, but perhaps even a fear and foreboding as to where the love of God might lead us. It would not merely be pastorally beneficial if the Lund principle were applied creatively to the life of the less populous communities of the country. Undoubtedly, new questions of communal justice and integrity would begin to intrude into public consciousness. But these are the very things that people seek most to evade. As the chorus in T S Eliot's *Murder in the Cathedral* lamented, we are, for the most part, the kind of people who want to shut out our innermost fears as we close the door and sit huddled by the fire. We fear the blessing of God with the surrender that this requires; indeed, 'we fear the injustice of men less than the justice of God'. We fear anything and everything less than we fear the love of God.

But perhaps we must begin by trusting that the lay members of the church are indeed more adult than the leadership of the church will allow them to be; indeed, 'growing up' may be the first task facing the church of post-Catholic Ireland. Christ's teaching resonates throughout with the reminder that those who seek only survival will lose the life they treasure so much. Those who are more generous and giving, and who are heedless of their own survival, will grow and prosper. The call to the church of today is to re-examine and re-evaluate the structures to which it clings so dearly. Nothing in the organisation of the church has any more importance than the degree to which it enables ministry to flourish. The structures are there as the tools of mission and ministry. If they are proving less than adequate to that purpose, they are dispensable.

The Lund principle needs therefore to be taken more seriously than ever before. Only when there is the recognition that there is indeed a common nucleus to the Christian faith, that there are specific beliefs within which all Christians can find common ground and through which they can acknowledge one another as fellow-Christians (even if not of the same tradition), can the Lund principle take root. This may perhaps be accomplished not so much by earnest documents as by shared action, and one of the giant leaps the church must take is in translating its cold knowledge of doctrine into an active love. T S Eliot wrote of our losing wisdom in knowledge, as we lose knowledge in information, but it was the fourteenth century mystic Walter Hilton who gave this transfiguration of knowledge into the wisdom of love its deepest dimension, in the quiet heart of God:

By itself knowledge is like water,
tasteless and cold.
Lord Jesus, I offer this knowledge humbly to you,
and ask for your grace.
Turn the water into wine with your blessing
as you did at the request of your mother
at the marriage feast.
By the gift of your Holy Spirit,
turn this savourless knowledge into wisdom,
and cold naked reason into spiritual light
and burning love.[9]

It can be done. I have written elsewhere in enthusiastic language of the Sant' Egidio Community. Founded over thirty five years ago in Rome by a young student who believed that he and his friends would achieve much by studying the Bible together, it is still a vibrant and energetic movement, spread now over more than sixty countries. Principally a lay movement and led by laity, it has nevertheless a strong sense of church and of the meaning of catholicity in its fullest sense. Although Roman Catholic to the core, it is ecumenical in every way. Based on worship, prayer, and an evangelical fervour for the scriptures as the

---

9. Walter Hilton, *Ladder of Perfection*, I.4. *Praying with the English Mystics*, ed. Jenny Robertson, SPCK, 1990, p 75.

foundation of Christian discipleship, this movement seamlessly translates its spiritual foundation into decisive action, ranging from AIDS programmes in Africa, to peace-broking throughout the world, to the provision of soup kitchens on the streets of Rome itself. The key lesson to be learnt from Sant' Egidio is that spirituality and action are not separated aspects of a committed Christian discipleship; they belong together and they cannot be separated. It is surely in shared action and worship that the distinctions between different Christians take their rightful place, as entirely secondary to a shared discipleship in the service of Christ. It is only when the different traditions in Ireland work together in the spirit of a Sant' Egidio community that the differences between them will assume their proper insignificance, and the church may become what it is meant by Christ to be, one Body with different limbs and organs, each requiring one another for the good of the whole.

CHAPTER NINE

Mending Our Ways

In a consumer culture which so prizes *choice*, any public institution must have a keen eye on its image. An institution which wishes *to be chosen* must appear attractive, or at least convincing. If we are honest, today's church is constantly tempted into seeking a makeover of its public image, finding ways of making itself cosmetically more attractive. For too long, Emily Dickinson's picture of a particular face she knew might as readily be applied to the appearance of the Irish church:

A face devoid of love or grace
A hateful, hard, successful face,
A face for which a stone
Would feel as thoroughly at ease
As were they old acquaintances –
First time together thrown.[10]

We may indeed use the skills and arts of public relations experts, media advisers and management consultants to ensure that the church looks better to the modern eye. But all would be style. Little would be real content. The church would very quickly be uncovered, and despised for its lack of integrity and a vacuum in substance. Indeed there is much to suggest that the brittleness of the church's public engagement with the world has already been well and truly uncovered by friend and foe alike. How, then, can we truly mend our ways and undergo a transformation which is more than an over-abundance of ecclesiastical make-up? I would want to suggest that there are three 'places' which the church of post-Catholic Ireland must explore, if there is any real desire to move beyond a mere change of image.

---

10. Emily Dickinson, *The Complete Poems*, 1711, Faber and Faber, 1975, p 695.

The first is a new emphasis on intellectual coherence. There is still a strong element, even within the church, which is ready to accept that one will hold to religious faith, *despite* one's intellect. An Anglican bishop of the seventeenth century, Edward Stillingfleet, once made the observation that Christians should have a faith which would move mountains, but not one which would swallow them. The Christian gospel is not contrary to reason, to common sense, or to intelligence. If religion is only for the non-thinking part of the human person, it is exceptionally dangerous. A religion which is only 'of the head' is defective; a faith which ignores the head is an invitation to spiritual schizophrenia.

We are already fully aware of a widely held assumption – sometimes but not always verbalised – that Christians do not really believe all the content of their faith. Sometimes the observer who makes such a comment is parodying (intentionally or unintentionally) what Christians do actually believe, but this is not always the case. The church of today is still left with the immense challenge of defending Christianity intellectually, yet without watering it down so that it becomes devoid of any objective content (and might hence be believed or disbelieved by anyone with an equal justification). Elsewhere I have sought to argue that Christianity is neither irrational nor intellectually puny, but the question in this context is more concerned with the degree to which the church today will accept the necessity to argue for the Christian faith as being, objectively, a reasonable proposition. If it will not, then it will indeed be despised as a refuse for fantasists who do not have the courage to accept the reality of their own mortality.

Today we have a generation of young people who, across the board, have been educated to higher levels than would, a generation earlier, have seemed possible. Many young people are simply better educated than their parents or, if not better educated, then certainly *further* educated. They have been encouraged and even forced to use their minds as an essential tool for understanding the world in which they live. To be confronted by a repository of non-material, spiritual ideas – ideas which those who propogate will not regard as requiring any rational defence whatsoever – will do little to convince any hard-headed young adult.

If a young person were even slightly impressed by an avowedly anti-intellectual approach to religious commitment, it would then follow that any particular religious package can only be a matter for individual taste. The entire post-modernist project has no particular problem with such an approach to personal faith. Faith, like lifestyle, is a matter of personal preference, the only question being what may best 'work' for the individual, what may enable the individual to feel better about life or self. Religious faith and practice are hence neither right nor wrong, neither sensible nor foolish. If Christianity is to make the claim that it is a faith embedded in history rather than in wish-fulfilment, nostalgia or sentiment, it must be ready to justify its claim.

Being rooted in history is a notion which may have little resonance in an age which has no interest in history. But Christianity has an historical dimension in two distinct ways and, if it chooses to ignore this, it has very little else to offer the world around it. In the first place there are the events in what is technically called 'salvation-history', the events seen by our religious ancestors in the Hebrew and Judeo-Christian traditions as revealing the divine, acting decisively and definitively in specific moments in history that have been recorded in the Bible. From a Christian perspective, salvation history takes a final and ultimate form in the incarnation and in those events which stemmed from it, notably the crucifixion and resurrection of Jesus Christ. That this makes axiomatic sense is simply not true. The basics of Christianity need to be explained and justified, not only as pleasant or helpful, but as believable by intelligent people. It is true that historical investigation and literary analysis will only carry the searcher some of the way towards committed faith. Sooner or later there must be the decisive personal step into a full commitment to the faith, a step which (having been taken) will then justify the commitment as it is lived out, but this necessary progression should never allow the church to sidestep the task of explaining the essentials of the Christian faith intelligently and cogently to all who will listen.

There is also a second sense in which Christianity is centred in the flow of history. The history of Christian disciples, both individually and within the community of the church, is a major part of what the church is today. People may indeed find part of this Christian history repellent – the Crusades, the Inquisition, the espousal and defence of slavery, and the religious wars which have stretched into our own generation are scarcely to the eternal credit of the church. Our history has nevertheless made us what we are and we cannot begin our reality now, however much we might wish to do so. Nor may we make any notional jump back to the early church, and believe ourselves to be in that setting again. The old cliché that those who ignore history will be doomed to repeat its mistakes may be applied with particular force to the Christian Church. In our generation (as in every generation), we enter into Christian history, the Christian story, some of which is glorious and some of which is atrocious. We have to take our place within that story, seeking to find our way beyond that which we cannot believe to be wholesome, but also learning humbly from the beauty and the glory of Christian lives that have reflected the light of Christ. This, in its own way, is what Pope John Paul II clearly sought to do, both with the canonisation of numerous saints and also in his apologies for horrors inflicted on the world by the church in previous generations. At times these actions seemed naïve to many, both outside and inside the Roman Catholic Church, but the principle is one on which all must stand. We are what we are because of history.

The task of the Christian Church, in Ireland as elsewhere, in an age which wishes to consign history to the junkheap of irrelevance, is to redeem history and to make sense of history, but without any attendant self-justification. We cannot understand any religious faith without locating it in its history and tradition. This is especially true of Christianity, as also of those other faiths of 'the Book', Judaism and Islam. If we seek to have Christianity without history, and without an intelligent and coherent understanding of that history (both the salvation history of the scriptures and the history of the Christian community), Christianity becomes only what we wish it to be. It becomes what we find attractive, and we simply excise the bits we do not wish to retain. The logical coherence of Christianity cannot become a luxury, of value only for those who wish to enjoy intellectual enquiry. The spirited defence of Christianity's reasonableness and intellectual honesty is the task for all Christian disciples today.

If a ruthless honesty about what we are as church, failures as well as accomplishments, is to be at the top of any agenda of righteousness today, a second area of re-alignment is that the church must be where reality is. In a book written over thirty years ago, *The Crucified God*, Jürgen Moltmann outlined five areas within modern society to which Christians must seek to relate the gospel. We might expect such a list to be very much out-of-date, but in fact it might have been tailor-made (with one small adaptation) to the setting of Ireland today. Moltmann's five areas were poverty, institutionalised violence (which we might wish to expand to all 'societal violence'), racism, the environment, and people's sense of meaninglessness. Yet the church – for the most part – is not to be found in such places.

I have long had a huge admiration for the Italian-Jewish writer Primo Levi, one of the few survivors of Auschwitz who was able to write with a degree of both objectivity and compassion about his experiences. In his book of essays, *The Periodic Table*, Levi tells of a Dr Müller who had been in charge of the laboratory in which he, Levi, had worked as a prisoner during the war. Levi had no hatred for Müller, more a curiosity about him, because he was probably, Levi reckoned, typical of many around him. The common technique, Levi writes, was to try to know as little as possible and therefore not to ask questions. Müller, says Levi, had obviously not asked questions of anyone, not even from himself, although from his laboratory window, clearly visible, were the flames of the crematorium at

Auschwitz. The Irish church cannot pretend it does not know what is happening around it today, and if the church cannot live and love inside the places of fear, degradation and need, it is still living in the sad delusions of Christendom. Christendom marked the association of church and state in coalition. The former supported the latter; the latter protected the former. As has already been outlined, post-Catholic Ireland means a post-Christendom Ireland.

As the years have passed and Irish men and women are able to reflect on what the fabled 'celtic tiger' actually did for the country we see things that were good, but other things that have proved injurious. We are now surrounded by people who do not 'have a life'. Many married couples work many miles away from their place of employment, and face hours of travel every weekday. The cost of housing in or near the main cities, Dublin in particular, has risen to such a degree that people who work in a city will spend almost no time in their own home, at times (literally) at home only for bed and breakfast. The quality of life for individuals and for families has been shredded. The sense of community in country towns within commuting range of Dublin or any of the other major cities, no longer exists.

If the church exists for any earthly function, it is to provide and to sustain community. Over seventy years ago, T S Eliot saw the vast, terrifying and apocalyptic vacuum at the heart of modern urban living without God. Since his time, little has changed for the better, and much for the worse. We indeed need to ask – as Eliot bids us in one of his choruses from 'The Rock' – whether, when his 'stranger' asks us what the meaning of our city may be, we huddle closer together because we genuinely love one another as community, or whether the unpalatable truth is rather that 'we all dwell together to make money from each other.'

And where there is a materialist prosperity there is a concomitant precariousness. The Irish economy (for all the eloquent denials by those in political power) is heavily dependent on globalisation and the multi-national economy. What has been given to Ireland in terms of investment may as readily be taken away, were a better financial deal to be found elsewhere. It is true that Ireland appears to provide an attractive site for the multi-national corporation in that it has produced a good balance between an attractive corporate tax system and an educated work-force, but there is still an underlying insecurity about all employment.

It is equally certain that the traditional Irish economy has changed beyond recognition and, as a concomitant, so has the traditional Irish community. As people have moved away from the country areas to the larger conurbations, and as farming becomes less labour intensive and less profitable, the traditional farming 'community' exists more in name than in reality. There is undoubtedly a deep dis-ease among many people, a dissatisfaction with what life is. This *ennui* may remain inarticulate but it is no less cancerous for that.

If there is a deep-seated unhappiness in many people who are somehow remaining on the carousel of economic success, there is acute need and deprivation among many who have become, in social and economic terms, an underclass in Irish society. We have no moral right merely to complain that there is a huge drug crisis, that some parts of the country have become virtual no-go areas for policing, or that teenage crime has reached epidemic proportions. We have together created such a society – a condition where, if there is no hope, alternatives will inevitably be found in a sub-culture of dysfunctionality. Recent assessments have shown that the Irish Republic, for all its proud boasts of success, has greater divisions between poverty and affluence than most other countries in Europe. In Ireland, the rich have every incentive and opportunity to become richer. The truly poor and disadvantaged appear to face a prospect only of further poverty and hopelessness.

The church's moral probity must be shown not merely in badgering government or the fortresses of economic power, although it must indeed be fearless and relentless in this. We begin with ourselves. The re-building of community and a sense of self-dignity and self-worth for all people is a primary task for the Christian community. If the church is to point beyond a crude consumerism – a consumerism which (it must be said) has only recently become a primary aspect of the Irish psyche – it must itself show a greater indifference to its own wealth and belongings. Indeed only when we are able to give away our treasures are those possessions not in fact our possessors. Only when we have the freedom to sell or give away those things we proudly regard as our religious heritage have they they any religious significance. The church can only preach what it does.

A third (and perhaps the most contentious) suggestion for a transformation of the church's life is that it should seek to be aesthetically attractive. This may seem to smack of elitism. That the church as an institution should be sincere, intelligible and honourable may seem obvious, but we need to look further and deeper to justify the contention that it should also be aesthetically appealing. A reasonable starting point is Jesus Christ's insistence that there are in fact actions which are beautiful, and which do not require any further justification or explanation. When a woman of dubious character lavished a great deal of money anointing him with perfume, Jesus tells his followers that she has done a beautiful thing. It is Judas Iscariot who complains that the money should have been used to alleviate poverty (John 12:1-8). Also in John's gospel, Our Lord describes himself as the good shepherd (10:11) which – if we follow the original Greek – would have meant a beautiful or attractive shepherd rather than a good shepherd in the sense either of competence or of moral character.

If we then are to argue that the church in its actions should be aesthetically engaging, the outworking of this begins with the way the church does liturgy. It is absurd to suggest that the only appropriate worship is what would characteristically be thought of as a cathedral style of worship – a liturgy which is extremely formal, dignified, and stylised with a strong emphasis on music sung by a choir rather than as suitable for congregational singing. This may indeed be an aesthetic feast and may also, for some people, be the best way in which they can approach and worship a God of beauty and transcendence. For others elaborate worship is simply a distraction from the immediacy of a God who came among his people in simple and unaffected form. There are important lessons here for the church to learn. It is one thing for worship to be accessible only to a minority of people. (It is also, incidentally, a mistake to believe that people who can appreciate very stylised or formalised worship are either aloof or insincere.) But the opposite extreme is also in error. To believe that any worship may be slovenly and ill-prepared is surely an insult to God and a congregation.

In recent years, it became *de rigueur* in all the traditions in Ireland to make worship accessible in the sense of doing liturgy in a way that was not stuffy, and within which people would feel relaxed and at ease. This has rightly been regarded as a particular necessity with regard to young people. But mistakes were undoubtedly made in pursuit of a good intention. Ease of manner tipped over into a gauche casualness with the things of God. Detailed preparation for a service was seen as patronising the congregation, in that spontaneity would be sacrificed. But it cannot be pretended that very many people have been impressed or brought into the community of the church by flippant and inarticulate preaching, repetitive banal prayers and a running commentary on what is really 'happening' in the words of worship.

The careful preparation of worship is essential. There is nothing in the scriptures to suggest that a lack of reverent attention to worship glorifies God, rather the opposite. And – when it comes to spontaneity – it need scarcely be said that the most effective 'art' is when the technique and artistry are not immediately obvious. The very best of seemingly 'impromptu' addresses are often the most rigorously prepared! Many years ago, I served part of my apprenticeship as a young priest in a parish which placed huge emphasis on presenting liturgy with great care. What one discovered was that, if the liturgy was properly prepared, the worship itself was not only beautiful but – simply because of the amount of diligent preparation – the celebrant, choir and congregation were able to submerge themselves into the worship of God without stress. There was none of the anxiety of wondering what was going to happen next, or when the next explanation or announcement would have to be made to straighten out mistakes on someone's part! The attention to detail went to the extreme of ensuring that the clergy and choir appeared through the doors of the sacristy as the clock in the tower was striking the hour. If people arrived late, they knew for sure that they were going to miss the beginning of the service. This may indeed seem unnecessarily fastidious, but few things can more convince the people of God of the profound importance of worshipping God with reverence and care than a meticulous preparation by those appointed to lead the worship. Well-prepared worship will inevitably create the right atmosphere, the precise mode or tradition of the worship itself notwithstanding. Such worship will not fail to be attractive and compelling in its impact.

What people of every age demand, and have a right to expect, is that worship will be done well. This involves making the worship something so real and vibrant that the unattached individual coming into a church, perhaps having given up their faith long before, perhaps indeed giving Christianity one last chance, may realise that this is indeed for real. There is the very famous story that, when he became ruler of the state which was later to be Russia in the late tenth century, Prince Vladimir of Kiev decided that he could unite his people far better if he could find one single religion for all of them. He sent envoys around the world to find the faith that best suited his country and people. Travelling from place to place they visited different peoples at worship – non-Christian as well as Christian – wondering whether any would be suitable for the Russians. Finally, they visited the city of Constantinople and attended worship in the great cathedral of Santa Sophia. One of the first Russian chronicles, *The Story of the Passing Years*, describes the experiences of those Russian envoys in Constantinople and the report they brought back: 'We did not know whether we were in heaven or earth, for upon earth there is no such sight or beauty; we only know that there, God is present among men.' The rest, proverbially, is history: in 988, Vladimir introduced Byzantine Christianity to Russia. It should surely be said of any act of Christian worship that those present do not know whether they are in heaven or earth but only that there, God is present among his people.

What is to be said of worship which is not only immediate and authentic but also attractive to the senses and to the mind may be applied equally to the words of liturgy, the music of liturgy and the place of liturgy. What is elaborate is not necessarily beautiful. What is simple is not necessarily less than beautiful. One need only step inside the Pantheon in Rome to see where the ultimate in simplicity may also be overwhelming in its impact.

It would indeed be futile if any new emphasis on an intellectual toughness in presentation of the gospel, an honest identification with the places of deprivation, or an aesthetic beauty in style, were pursued only as cosmetic repair work, the production of a more attractive or acceptable image for the church. The Irish church has undoubtedly damaged itself in its neglect of these aspirations, any of which should most surely be characteristics of any church which means to do serious business in the name of Christ. But as it seeks to repair the damage it has inflicted upon itself, it must move humbly and attentively. Otherwise it will assuredly impale itself on the twin spears of self-aggrandisement and self-delusion, for it is grace alone which may allow such purposes of mind, heart and beauty to penetrate anew the souls of men and women.

CHAPTER TEN

Faiths and Faith

As we gaze in astonishment at the Ireland of today, what we see is a multi-racial, multi-cultural, multi-faith society which demands that we find new ways of living together as different races, cultures or faiths, not just for today but into the long-term future. We must surely assume that the days of a culturally monolithic Ireland have gone for ever, and yet we must recall that this is something new. Until the final decade of the twentieth century, religious faith in Ireland meant simply an indigenous Christian faith, with some awareness of the small Jewish community which, although small, has been of long-standing, respected and visible presence. As a society we must now learn (and quickly) what it is to mean for us all, if we are to live well in this strange and unfamiliar place of multi-cultural faith and non-faith.

The religious landscape, even within the Christian Church, has of course changed enormously. Today, as fewer Irish-born people are showing any interest in the practice of the Christian faith, the wave of immigration in the wake of the upturn in the Irish economy has also meant that other expressions of Christianity are now highly visible and are becoming ever more visible on the Irish scene. This has given post-Catholic Ireland new vantage points from which to comprehend a Christian faith which is not bounded by the limitations of ethnic Irishness.

With regard to the latter, Christians of all traditions are aware of different expressions of the faith in their own tradition through the arrival into Ireland of Christians from the African continent. Roman Catholics, Anglicans, Methodists, and Presbyterians have all encountered different ways of expressing their faith, and no longer restricted by the limitations of the culture which they have always known in Ireland. To our shame, the Irish-born have not always given the warm welcome which should have been offered to Christians from other backgrounds. The welcome has no doubt often been along the lines (even subliminally) of, 'Welcome to our church provided that you fit in with our way of doing things.'

Irish liturgies have no doubt seemed formalised, lifeless, and lacking in the spontaneity which is integral to Christian worship – in all its traditions – in Africa. In Ireland we are obsessed with time, and do not expect our Sunday worship to continue for too long; we have very western ideas about arriving on time and of not spending too long at worship. In a previous generation, the sermon – certainly in the reformed traditions – was a centrepiece within worship, and the sermon or homily might well last for half an hour or more without complaint from any of the congregation. This was the expectation. Today a sermon which runs for longer than ten or twelve minutes is regarded as garrulous. Many African arrivals in Ireland are deeply surprised by the reluctance of Irish Christians to spend more than one hour (and preferably far less) in church on a Sunday morning. Although Irish people may indeed try to be welcoming and to show hospitality, this is circumscribed by the intense 'privacy' with which people in western society today now guard their homes, their time and their families. An Irish man or woman may indeed ask a new acquaintance to 'call in on them' whenever they are in the neighbourhood. Whereas thirty or forty years ago (particularly in rural areas) this would have been intended to be taken literally, today it is not. As the sense of community has eroded, the circle of casual friends for most people has reduced. The hospitality we offer to all but a small circle of friends has become more organised, less spontaneous, and by specific invitation only. The sad truth is that many African Christians do not feel truly welcome within congregations and parishes here. They believe that, if they are indeed welcomed, it is entirely subject to the strict condition that they conform to the local Irish practice and expectations. A welcome which is grudging or attached to conditions is not true hospitality. The consequence has been that a number of African Christians have now segregated into worshipping communities of their own, believing that there they can 'be themselves' with no disapproval or condescension. The Christian Church as a whole has been the loser. We might all learn a great deal about Christianity (and about ourselves) if we had the opportunity to experience our own Christian tradition outside the context in which we have always known it. Inevitably our own understanding of Christianity is limited by the degree to which our context has shaped it.

It may not yet be too late to retrieve the situation, and somehow to integrate the worship of African and Irish Christians within the same worship. It may be a matter of both/and. After all, if we wish to see value in the fact that we are not all of the same tradition, this has implications within our traditions also. It may be valuable to worship together sometimes, but also to allow that different people will wish to worship in differing ways, and that this is not of itself an indication of failure. What would be failure would be a form of unspoken apartheid, operating in both directions, which makes it clear that we do actually prefer the company of people whom we regard as being 'like us', because they are of the same ethnic background. If African and Irish Christians are to witness to a common faith, it will only be when each is humble and attentive to the expectations, the spiritual needs and even the foibles of the other. We would undoubtedly all be given more than we would give, and would discover that any sacrifices we had made were repaid by what we had received.

Another unfamiliar feature on the new Irish Christian landscape is the arrival of Orthodox Christians, principally from eastern Europe. Between the census years of 1996 and 2002, the number of Orthodox Christians in the Republic of Ireland increased several times over. As with the arrival of African Christians, this also gives opportunities for a general and wholesome rediscovering of Christianity, and for expanding Christian horizons for Ireland. The Roman Catholic and reformed traditions in Ireland have of course been aware of the Orthodox tradition for centuries, but largely as something distant and exotic which we possibly admired, but without being quite sure what we were admiring! Orthodox congregations in Ireland, particularly in Dublin, are expanding and are drawing converts from other Christian traditions, and from those who had lapsed from all religious faith. Although the relationship of the Orthodox communions to the western traditions has, over the centuries, been one of varying warmth and coldness, the Irish setting has been almost entirely warm. Irish Christians of the western traditions have realised that here is an expression of the faith which is focused intensely both on liturgy and on theology. We have been reminded, by the visible presence of the Orthodox tradition in our midst, of what worship is truly about, the glory of God. People of all traditions thus have the opportunity of being brought back to priorities and spiritual realities they had relinquished. What is more crucial than ever before is that the despisers of all religion may see different traditions of Christianity living and working in harmony and co-operation with one another, rather than as competing enterprises seeking to out-do one another in a bid to attract customers.

But the religious landscape has grown far beyond the specifically Christian vista. In the Republic of Ireland, Muslims outnumber Methodists. The Christian traditions are now required to decide (and quickly) on their attitude to those who are deeply religious, but who are not Christian. A generation or two ago, the direct and simple answer would have been that the duty of the Christian Church was to convert to Christianity those of other religious faiths. Today this would be a minority view. Religious proselytisation is regarded as the worst kind of arrogance. Distinctions are sometimes made between what are called the 'Abrahamic faiths' (Judaism, Christianity and Islam), and those of other religious faiths. Adherents to any of the three Abrahamic faiths may also regard themselves as having a common ground not only in the figure of Abraham, but as 'People of the Book', people whose understanding of divine revelation is, partially at least, rooted in a common book, the Hebrew Bible, for all that it is understood, developed and interpreted in such different ways within the different faith-traditions.

We are encouraged to understand more of one another's faiths, particularly in a world where antagonisms and violence seem to be the prevalent hallmarks of religious faiths. In the post-9/11 world, we are more and more conscious of different religious cultures. This is a world where many Muslims see Christians as being still in 'crusade' mode, wishing the destruction of Islam, by violent means if necessary. It is a world where many Christians fear Islam, choosing to see and hear only words and actions of violence, and preferring to believe that this is the true basis of the Islamic faith. This is also a world where many Jews in the state of Israel believe that they have no friends, and that they must attack Palestinian Muslims and Christians if they are to survive. It is far too easy to dismiss such attitudes, from all these religious faiths, as mere misinterpretation of religious faith. But the only way to remove misinterpretation is to dialogue with one another, and with the utmost of humility and with genuine trust. Indeed, one of the most important reasons why respectful dialogue must be encouraged is in order that Christians, Jews and Muslims may together seek to understand the relationship between religious faith and violence. None of the Abrahamic faiths can claim that its history and even some of its own internal tradition is not steeped in human blood. Until the faiths can come to terms with what this means to the world of today, there will always be those who will find that they must reject all religious faith because it appears to be less wholesome, and certainly more violent, than a compassionate atheism.

But, if we are to move beyond the superficial misunderstanding of one another's faiths, what is the common ground on which we stand? There is clearly – within Judaism, Christianity and Islam – a common monotheistic belief in the God of Abraham. But for a believing Jew, Christianity is monstrously deluded at its very core; for the Jewish believer, Jesus of

Nazareth cannot be truly divine. The Muslim, similarly, cannot believe that Jesus Christ is true God and true man, however great a prophet he may have been. For the Christian who takes the faith seriously, Judaism is incomplete, and Islam has gone beyond the belief that salvation is to be found in Christ, and that his life, death, and resurrection represents the entire revelation of God. In the interests of mutual understanding, there must never be a watering down of what each faith actually stands for. And there is a further conceptual chasm which cannot be explained away in the interests of tolerance. For all that Christians rightly understand themselves as 'People of the Book', there is also in Christianity the foundational understanding of the Word of God as a person, Jesus Christ. For Jews and Muslims, the Word of God is the Book.

If the relationship between the Abrahamic faiths is to move beyond a superficial acceptance that all three faiths believe in one God and that all have respect – albeit in differing ways – for the Hebrew Bible, there must be a clarity about religious conviction, and there must be a total commitment to the beliefs which stem from this conviction. If we have an existential commitment to the particular religious faith by which we live, we cannot regard all religious faith (or even Abrahamic religion specifically) in simple generic terms, or as a smorgasbord from which to take whatever may suit, while regarding other choices as, essentially, other preferences from within the same menu. To draw a line between patronising indifferentism and truculent proselytisation is far from easy. The crucial truth is that if religious convictions are not held with utter commitment, there is little to offer to others.

Yet, while holding passionately to these convictions, there must surely be a value in a wholesome and respectful relationship with other faiths. One of the saddest developments in Christianity is that religious faith – for most post-enlightenment Christians (however devout they may be) – is often but one 'compartment' within a wider life. There is a lack of connection between faith as expressed in worship and private devotion, and life as it is lived on a daily basis. For Muslims there is no such compartmentalisation. Political life, family life, social life and business life are all incorporated into faith. Traditional Jewish family life is equally an integral part of religious life. The modern western Christian, of whatever tradition, can only be enriched by a humble engagement with those faiths which have not lost their way of seeing life, in all its aspects, as a single unity under God. It need not be patronising for Irish Christians to discover from their new Muslim neighbours that at the heart of a religious faith is a God who is sovereign. The casual picture of a God who may at times be ignored, and at other times summoned for our use or necessity, would rightly be regarded as blasphemy by the Muslim. It should be seen as equally blasphemous for Christians to think and act in this way. The Christian Church in today's Ireland needs to be reminded of the truth that if God *is*, he is supreme over every aspect of life, and demands worship and obedience in every situation. Similarly, a wholesome engagement with Judaism in a proper spiritual environment recalls any thinking Christian to the true vision of the founder of Christianity as thoroughly Jewish. One cannot love the God revealed in Christ, and despise Judaism. Indeed it is only when we are at ease with our Jewish ancestry that Christianity can ever be encountered in all its beauty and richness. The danger of this is that we may become condescending to those of other faiths, and be patronisingly grateful to them for reminding us of the fuller implications of our own faith. This is not what religious dialogue means. Much, although not all of what has been said with regard to the Abrahamic faiths, may readily be transferred to other religious faiths. Already there are many Irish-born converts to Buddhism, who have found that the faith of their birth no longer answers the questions that Buddhism can satisfy.

Although there is a genuine ease with the older traditional world faiths that are not Abrahamic (such as Buddhism, Hinduism or Shintoism), there is huge reluctance to accept the dignity of more modern faiths, which we promptly dismiss as cults or sects. The dividing line between a cult and a religious faith is never easy to draw. There is a widespread abhorrence of religious groups which seem to rely on techniques akin to brainwashing. The despisers of all religion would of course throw precisely the same accusation at the mainstream faiths. Perhaps all that is required is that only those faith-communities from which the individual may in conscience freely withdraw without persecution are to be regarded as suitable for truthful interfaith dialogue. The contentious matter of 'sharing prayer' with those of other faiths then becomes more secure. We are all undoubtedly praying to God but, thankfully, not to a God of our possession. We are praying to a God whom we all seek to serve, but recognising at the same time that we cannot all be equally 'right' in how we see God. We pray that God in his eternal wisdom and love may through the wholeness of the religious pilgrimage, in time or out of time, correct all that is amiss in our clouded vision.

As Ireland becomes less religiously monolithic, other questions must arise. If it is not necessary to be Roman Catholic in order to consider oneself as 'fully Irish', can one be 'fully Irish' and Muslim, or 'fully Irish' and Hindu? Our neighbours in Britain have faced such a question for several generations. The answer is that some of those who came to Britain from other cultures and faiths assimilated completely into the British way of life without reneging on their expression of faith. Younger generations, however, have wished to stress their distance from the surrounding British culture. In France, where many of an older generation of Muslims have assimilated almost entirely into the French environment, it is younger Muslims (teenagers and schoolchildren) who have demanded that they be allowed to express their religious beliefs more openly, as in, for example, their dress code. We must become aware that if the notion of a national culture that is not coterminous with a specific religious faith is novel to Ireland, such a vision is also anathema to some of other faiths. The idea of a neutral, secular or pluriform culture is not the norm in many Islamic states. This is not a matter for praise or blame. It is a reality with which Ireland as a whole must learn to do business. We cannot assume that those who have come to our country from outside will necessarily wish to adapt to our existing culture. Indeed, what constitutes 'Irishness' at any point in time is what Ireland actually *is*, not what we might wish it to be. Too many lives have been destroyed in the vain and foolish attempt to locate full Irishness in some never-never land of the past or of the future. Those who were born in Ireland have no monopoly on defining Irish identity. It will become what it will become. It will never again be what it has been in the past. We must live in the world as it is, and not in the fictitious world that has gone for ever. As W H Auden expressed beautifully in his poem 'Another Time' (written in another disconcerting period of history, the first months of the Second World War), many people try to say 'Not Now', and many have forgotten how to say 'I Am', and 'would be lost, if they could, in history', bowing to 'a proper flag in a proper place, muttering like ancients as they stump upstairs, of Mine and His and Ours and Theirs.' Those days of 'mine' and 'his' and 'ours' and 'theirs' in Ireland have gone for ever.

Yet what is essential is that the church, and all people of goodwill, show a tolerance towards those who wish to maintain, within Irish society, a distinctive religious or cultural identity with which we are not familiar. The only demand we may justifiably make is that an equal moderation is shown to us and to future generations. The Irish church, in particular the Church of Ireland, has talked glibly about 'pluralism' without having much idea about what it might come to mean. Now is the moment of truth, when we accept that Irish society will from now be multiform, and that this need not be a matter for fear.

The almost total collapse of the geo-political landscape in the years since 9/11 has shown just how horrifically and violently damaging the non-communication between different religious and ethnic cultures may become. Somehow all who wish to make the transition from Catholic Ireland to post-Catholic Ireland must together seek to establish what it is to be truly human in Ireland today, indeed, what 'humanism' is properly to mean.

I may, as a Christian believer, strongly uphold the gospel demand that Christ is to be proclaimed. May I not also believe that all – religious believer and non-believer, Christian, Jew, Muslim, Buddhist, agnostic or atheist alike – should gather together around a transformed model of 'humanism'? In our traditional culture, humanism is often understood only as an agnosticism which, although enthusiastic about humanity in general, is hostile to religious faith in all its forms. True humanism, as it would be understood in the mainstream of the European philosophical tradition, has no difficulty in finding as respected a place for the religious mind as for the wholly secularist mind. For the religious believer, this is not a denial or diminution of religious faith; it is a necessary engagement with the question which is crucial for the maturity and wisdom of all reflective people, whether of religious faith or of none – 'What does being human mean?' Different religious and non-religious traditions of thought may indeed find mutually incompatible answers to that question, but a shared tranquil space where we may live and speak safely may nevertheless be found.

The seeking of the space in which such an engagement may be undertaken, but without either uneasiness or an agenda of proselytisation, is an imperative for the whole world but also for individual societies such as the new Ireland. There is no convention in Ireland of any mutually respectful and sympathetic dialogue between faiths, or (more particularly) between faith and non-faith. We must begin before the disintegration of Irish society becomes irreparable.

There should indeed be a humble engagement of hearts and minds with those of other religious faiths. We do our own religious convictions no honour if we cannot set ourselves – through those very convictions – to speak with others and to learn from others, those of faith and those without religious faith, of an authentic humanism which seeks for the shared humanness of all around us in a new and different Ireland.

CHAPTER ELEVEN

The Frontiers of Orthodoxy

The poet Czeslav Milosz tells us forcefully that if God did indeed become incarnate, die and rise again from death, it follows that 'all human endeavours deserve attention only to the degree that they depend on this, i.e. acquire meaning thanks to this event'. If it be the case that the incarnation of the divine in Jesus Christ is the key to understanding all else (and, from the perspective of orthodox Christian belief it is difficult to suggest otherwise), the implications are surely clear: The details of Christian belief must matter. This may be the obvious implication but, in the Ireland of today, it is also highly problematic. Why?

We take as axiomatic the belief that the church of post-Catholic Ireland must somehow be enabled to present the claims of Christianity effectively and persuasively. And there is, in consequence, an inevitable desire by many within the church to make Christianity appear as inclusive as is possible. This is for a number of reasons. First, many have rejected Christianity because the church has appeared to be irredeemably excluding in its demands. Belonging to the church meant signing on to a fairly tight set of regulations and restrictions and much of this seemed to sit uneasily with all that the founder of Christianity stood for. Jesus Christ was noted for his openness to others, and for an intense dislike of pettiness and exclusiveness. Much of the distaste for the church in today's Ireland is rooted in the belief that the church in its worldly pursuit of power and control has made Christianity far narrower and stricter than its founder would ever have countenanced. There is therefore every temptation to make Christianity so accommodating, as for the word 'Christianity' to mean anything or nothing. The beliefs of Christianity would thus become far less important than that more people accepted the description 'Christian' for themselves. Christian belief – what constitutes Christian orthodoxy (the word itself meaning 'right belief') – would have no discernible definition of any kind. Indeed the word orthodoxy has already become almost like Humpty Dumpty's glory – a word which can be taken as meaning whatever we wish it to mean. In the case of 'orthodoxy', this usually simply signifies the self-belief of the individual who uses the word. It is also used as a cipher to exclude all others whose views are held to be unsound; in short, 'If you do not agree with me, you are not orthodox.'

Orthodoxy has become even more problematical for the church of today for another reason – there is a far greater concern with the other side of the coin in Christian living, what is sometimes called *ortho-praxis*, right conduct or right behaviour. Being a Christian is often taken to mean a way of living, and little else. In other words, the virtues of generosity, unselfishness and sacrificial love are understood as the real components of a Christian life. The precise nature or content of belief is not only secondary but a matter of relative unconcern. Indeed, if a life reflects virtue, the belief or lack of belief underlying such virtue is of no consequence. If the individual concerned wishes to apply the title 'Christian' for his or her beliefs, no-one else may suggest that this may not be appropriate. Such an attitude is very much part of the entire post-modernist era. It might be summarised as, "'Truth' is what I find useful to accept as 'truth' and if my idea of truth is what I claim I have derived from my 'take' on Christianity, I have a perfect right to call it Christian and you have no right to say that it is not Christian.' This however seems to fly in the face of logic and of language.

In the first place, Christianity is not merely a code of practice. Christ's teaching is undoubtedly a call to sacrificial love. But it is more than this. Christ also calls his followers into a relationship with God which involves specific beliefs; the call to righteousness is far more a call to be in a relationship with God, than the demand to do certain right things. Furthermore it is patronising in the extreme to assume that certain good behaviour can be classified *ipso facto* as Christian. An individual atheist may behave with great sacrificial nobility and generosity. His or her behaviour is not thereby 'Christian', and it is condescending not to see this good conduct for what it is – good living – without feeling any need to attribute it to Christian values. We may certainly describe certain actions as 'unChristian', but this only has much meaning if it is behaviour perpetrated by an individual claiming to be a Christian. To say that someone's behaviour is unBuddhist if he or she is not a Buddhist is not to say anything very meaningful.

But there is more to be considered. To use language with such looseness whereby we can call anything 'Christian', should we feel the urge so to do, makes all language redundant. If individuals living in Belfast wish to say that they live in Birmingham, because for them Belfast may realistically be regarded as Birmingham, they may presumably do so. It is not, however, a proper use of language. The demand for a new openness and understanding, when it comes to expressing Christianity in new ways, is crucially important. This should not mean, however, that language is to lose all meaning. Liberalism does not mean that there is no place for classification of any kind. One simply cannot say with any integrity that Christianity is a way of living and nothing more. Nor may one say with any intelligibility that Christianity may mean whatever an individual might find useful as a way of understanding God. If a particular vision of God turns out to be classically Buddhist, Islamic or Jewish, there is little sense in terming it as Christian. Even a post-modern world cannot expect the human race to eschew taxonomy completely.

Particularly in Anglican circles in the western world, there is also a fashion for what is called 'non-realism'. In brief, non-realism is the conviction that God is not an objective reality, independent of the human mind, but that he/she is a construct of human imagination. The non-realist would claim that God and religious language are not 'bad' constructs, unless they make people do bad things to others in the name of God or religion.

Indeed the language of religion may be very helpful in living a good life. But it is not based on an objective reality, on a God who is independent of us, and who would remain in existence even if the entire human race disappeared. God is, in other words, an idea which has value in enabling humanity to face life with purpose and focus. Religious language, with its timbre, its comfort and its hope, is helpful for people, but it does not denote any objective reality. Non-realism is mystifying to many of us. Compassionate atheism is worthy of an enormous respect from those who are believers. For an individual to say 'I believe that there is no God and that we humans are a chance accident of nature which is itself a chance accident, but I wish to do good to others and to place their needs before my own', is genuinely deserving of the humble respect and admiration of all. One is forced to ask why non-realists wish to employ the language of religion if it is not based on some objective reality. To have doubts and fears about the reality of God is one thing. To have resolved these doubts and fears, and decided that God is after all non-existent, but that the language of religion is pleasant and therefore usable, is surely to opt for the worst of all worlds. It seems to sacrifice intellectual coherence and integrity for no clear gain. Religious language is a different *genre* to the scientific language of the empirical, and if religion-speak is only a means to express the unrealisable longings and emotional yearnings of people who fully accept that their cravings are ultimately delusional, why not turn to poetry, even to the poetry of atheists? Religious language was not formulated by atheists. It seems condescending and arrogant to use the heartfelt language deriving from the sincere belief of believers in the transcendent God as a means for feeling good about life or self.

The church may well have blurred and distorted the vision of God for many people over many centuries. Many, inside and outside the church, may indeed have to struggle in order to maintain faith in a God of truth who seems at times barely discernible. Many stagger between dissatisfied belief and dissatisfied non-belief. Yet however we may wish to describe the

Christian faith and the God of the Christian vision, there must surely be a firm conviction that if God is ultimately our invention we must have the integrity to term ourselves as atheists and to take the spiritual consequences with a clear-eyed and honourable acceptance.

If we see belief in God as objective reality as a *sine qua non* for Christian orthodoxy, are there parameters to Christian belief which should equally be regarded as non-negotiables if the word 'Christianity' is to retain meaning in language? There are those who wish to make Christianity a faith which is narrowly circumscribed and which is restricted to particular forms of words in explanation. Some of this relates to the Bible. What is the relationship of the Bible to Christianity in all of its traditions? Clearly different traditions within the church place differing emphases on scripture. But for all Christian traditions there must be an affirmation that the Bible is uniquely authoritative in defining Christianity. We are still left with the question as to whether there is any single understanding of the role of the Bible which could encompass the whole Christian Church. Those who call themselves biblical literalists would certainly doubt that they had any common ground with the exponents of radical biblical criticism when it came to defining the place of the Bible in the life of the individual Christian disciple or of the Christian community. Some literalists regard those who treat the text of scripture as appropriate for human critical analysis as outside the ambit of the Christian community. There is of course some inconsistency in this. Any preaching of the scriptures is, in its own way, 'biblical criticism', in that it seeks to interpret scripture. Any interpretation of scripture necessarily involves some degree of critical method from the individual who undertakes it, regardless of whether that individual regards himself or herself as a traditionalist, a fundamentalist, a liberal or a radical.

There is, however, an important underlying issue here in the question of the status of the scriptures in the Christian understanding. If the scriptures are nothing more for the Christian than a set of ancient texts which are of interest for the understanding of God they display within the historical context in which they were written (and which may also contain some notable aphorisms and penetrating images) the Bible is more or less dispensable. The literalists and the liberals of the Christian Church should find themselves able to find a common ground around the proposition that the Bible is the 'Book of the Church', and in a unique and definitive way. The scriptures clearly did not descend from God in a single, complete and finalised volume descending from the heavens. It came from the communal experience of a people as they learnt more and more about the God whom they worshipped, and whom they believed had created them for a purpose. As to what was to be regarded as 'The Bible', this was not a decision conveyed to the church by direct divine command. Several centuries elapsed before the church made the final decision as to what should be contained within the New Testament and what should be excluded. The Hebrew Bible did not reach its final form without human discussion and debate, and nor did the New Testament. Christians believe that these decisions were made with the guidance of the Holy Spirit of God. They have no alternative but to believe that the Hebrew Bible, the Old Testament, also reached its finalised shape with the guidance of the Holy Spirit. But the truth remains that, no matter how traditionalist a view any individual may take of the status of the scriptures, it was flawed humanity which was involved both in the writing of the books which make up the Bible, and also in the decisions as to what would ultimately constitute the canonical scriptures. If we seek to suggest that those Christians of the third or fourth century who made the final decisions as to what precisely would constitute the Bible were infallible in their judgements, we are on very strange ground indeed.

It seems that if we are to steer a path between, on the one hand, the post-modernist individualism which says (in effect) that the real Bible is whatever the individual reader finds of use, and – on the other hand – the intellectually unsustainable contention that the scriptures were delivered verbatim by God (without intermediary human agency) directly to the church, we must acknowledge the firm presumption that the Bible *as it is* is elemental, primary and uniquely authoritative in defining Christianity. This is merely the beginning of the task of sharing the scriptures in ways which are not mutually exclusive. Some wish to use the scriptures in ways which emphasise the broad stroke of the message. Others wish to scrutinise every iota of text. What is surely essential is that we are not condescending to the Bible or to its writers.

If we move on from the place of God and the place of scripture in any assessment of what the non-negotiables in the definition of Christianity might be, we come to the person of Christ. Where are the frontiers in any Christian understanding of the incarnation? This question must be asked again today, not in any desire to reduce Christianity to restrictive formulae, but rather in the interests of clarity. Rather as with the understanding of God as non-contingent on the human mind, if the word 'Christianity' is to be used with any intelligibility, the place of Jesus Christ in relation to God requires some measure of definition. Many today admire the person of Jesus Christ. They would see him as a good man, perhaps even a great man, but in essence a prophet and nothing more. Is that belief sufficient to warrant the term 'Christian', even using the term in an entirely neutral sense? The understanding of Jesus Christ received by the church from its origins is that he was far more than a prophet. He was, fully and completely, within his person, God within humanity. To believe otherwise is to twist the meaning of straightforward language into absurd contortions. We have nevertheless still to ask whether or not the divine nature of Christ is a non-negotiable in any definition of 'Christianity'.

One of the first tasks set for any college student of theology or biblical studies to undertake is an examination of what may be a distinction between – to use the traditional terminology – the 'Jesus of history' and the 'Christ of faith'. The Jesus of history is the historical person, Jesus of Nazareth. We read of Jesus and his ministry in the New Testament gospels, but the question may legitimately be asked as to the extent to which the early Christians who wrote of him were influenced by the fact that they were writing from a new perspective, that which now saw him as the Christ, even as fully divine. Even unknowingly, did they distort the historical picture in order to emphasise beliefs about Jesus which had accrued after his departure from the earth, but which were in fact not rooted in the 'real' Jesus? Some students will come to the conclusion that the Jesus proclaimed in the gospels is the Jesus of history *and* the Christ of faith, in a total overlap and with no distinction. At an opposite end of the spectrum, there is a school of thought which argues that there is virtually nothing to be known about the real Jesus, the Jesus of history, and that the gospels should be read as beliefs of the early church community which may well have been far removed from most of what Jesus was, or what he understood himself to be.

Many in a middle ground, and I would place myself in such a place, are content to suggest that there is no feasible reason why a religion which makes such historical claims for itself would have been founded on an almost complete fabrication. The gospels were not, after all, compiled many centuries after the facts of Jesus' life were forgotten. In the first century environment, a generation – in terms of collective memory – was probably the equivalent of a week in the world of today. The gospels may not have been intended as snap-shot accounts of Jesus Christ's ministry but they are sufficiently close to the events they describe as to make them acceptable as largely factual rather than as theological fantasy. In other words, the Christ of history was sufficiently derived from the Jesus of history as to make the basics of the incarnation a core belief for his followers. To seek to dismiss the incarnation as 'mythology' in the sense of mere metaphor is to misuse the word myth. A myth is a means whereby the supernatural or superhuman is conveyed by way of story. The myth will normally be placed in a distant place and in a distant time from the telling of it. If the incarnation is to be regarded as myth, it must be such in the proper sense, not as a legend in the world of fiction but as a true story which nevertheless tells of transcendental realities. Such a story need not be fiction. As J R R Tolkien and C S Lewis discussed during the period of the latter's conversion to Christianity, the incarnation may reasonably assume the status of a 'true myth'.

Have we then to make the incarnation - the belief that Jesus is God and man – a non-negotiable in any reasonable definition of Christianity? It would seem that we have no alternative. There is an unbridgeable chasm between believing that Jesus was a good man, and believing that he reveals God within humanity to the world. In its own way, it is as massive a dislocation as between arguing that God is a human construct, and accepting that he is an objective reality, independent of human mind for existence. However we may wish to formulate an understanding of the incarnation, it must reasonably encapsulate the concept that Christ is in himself the definitive revelation of God within humanity. This was not God pretending to be human, nor was it a man whom people respected so much that they decided they should proclaim him as a god. Both of these are deeply unspiritual notions. In a way which defies rigorous formulae and human definition, the Christian belief is in Christ, truly, completely and objectively human and divine. The Christian faith goes on to proclaim that it is in a relationship with Jesus Christ that humanity, both as individuals and in community, can bridge the chasm between God and his creation. This reconciling of God and humanity, as God-ness and human-ness, are brought together in the person of Christ, and are centred on certain events in Jerusalem nearly two thousand years ago, when Jesus of Nazareth was crucified. Not only as symbol or metaphor but in a mysterious reality, God-ness and human-ness were reconciled. The depravity of which humankind was (and is) capable was not only matched but more than matched by the love of God. Whatever the resurrection of Christ was, it was an objective validation (and one must use the word 'objective' here also) of what Christ was and is. The idea that in some sense the resurrection was a fictional happy ending, added on to the grim story which had preceded it, makes no effort to explain why this should have been done. The stories of the resurrection are for the most part very restrained. Had this been the final scene in a contrived melodrama, the authors would surely have achieved far better results.

It may seem that some of this outline of the basics of orthodox Christian belief is both rather minimalist and written in language far removed from the credal statements of the church. There is no doubt that if the church were writing the creeds today, they would have been written differently. The concerns might have been different. The language would certainly have been different. This does not mean that the creeds may therefore be dismissed either as foolish speculation or as ecclesiastical truncheons with which to beat the sceptics. The intention of the creeds was to find the frontiers of what constituted Christianity. It is, however, one thing to seek to explain Christianity in language other than the historic creeds of the church but in terms which are consonant with them, and another to deny the importance of the creeds for understanding Christian belief, dismissing them as the efforts of people less intelligent or sophisticated than are we, and whose work we may therefore presume to 'correct'.

The post-modern world of today finds any ideas of definition inimical. It is regarded as unacceptable to exclude anyone or anything *from* anything. Without seeking to build ramparts around itself or to consign others to an outer darkness, can Christianity define itself in a way which must preclude some from claiming the name 'Christian'? If 'Christianity' is what anyone wishes it to mean, then the word simply has no meaning. I have suggested certain defining characteristics in the interests not of exclusion but of clarity. There are, after all, alternatives aplenty for those who have found another religious path. Unitarianism is there for those who love God but who cannot believe that Jesus has a status other than as a prophet. There are many converts in Ireland to Buddhism. There are Irish converts, fewer in number, to Islam although this number may well increase. If there is an alternative religious home for people who in conscience find that they must deny basic tenets of Christianity, there seems to be little need to demand that the definition of Christianity be stretched to the point of meaninglessness in order that they may no longer have to deny their Christianity.

But the church must still encourage the seeker, the uncertain, and the doubtful to join with the community of faith in a pilgrimage towards truth. The church is not merely a haven for the certain and the convinced. Even less is it a place for those who would wear their certainties as a badge of virtue, the self-righteous who have nothing in common with the righteous. Those who are able to believe fervently but without huge effort are not morally superior to those for whom every day is a struggle with faith. Those for whom faith is at times intensely difficult may well be closer to the heart of God, than is the smug 'insider' who has never thought deeply or cared at any depth.

The church does not have every answer nor should it claim to do so. It may be a conduit for Christian faith, but its behaviour too often belies the faith it proclaims. The good news is that God can make his own presence felt in the world without the churches; even more astonishingly, he can make his presence known in religious places which are insults to his love and his majesty.

Having noted that there was now an emphasis on orthopraxis which has overshadowed the importance of the content of the Christian faith, there is balance still to be found. If the church is seen as a place of vanity, of power-struggle and of pettiness, any message it may proclaim of the love of God will not be heard. What it is seen to be often drowns out what it has to say. The church as an institution often stumbles and flounders, and it is at times tired and weary and extremely foolish. The church does not contain the wholeness of all truth; it declares certain things it believes to be true about God. The church must welcome those who are able to find resonances – however faint and whispered those echoes may be – with what it is saying of God in Christ.

It must do so with humility as well as with love, for one may speak truth only with the greatest of care, perhaps only with a diffidence and shyness. Love and truth must be spoken with a reticence. And, within that essential humility, the church may also recall that Jesus spoke in parables, tangentially and indirectly, and that he did not speak about the church of God. He spoke of the kingdom of God.

The kingdom of God is the means of describing God's rule or God's sovereignty. The church is not the kingdom of God. It is set in the world to proclaim the kingdom. It is, albeit imperfectly, *of* the kingdom. There are cruel, obsessive and dysfunctional aspects within the church which are assuredly not of the kingdom of God. The kingdom may also be found far outside the walls of church, but the church must still seek to point towards the kingdom and to draw others to find their place within God's sovereignty, even if they never quite find a place inside the institutional church. But we must speak, with the quiet if reticent assurance of the truly Christ-like, of the conviction that all human endeavour attains its proper significance only when it is made dependent on a particular objective reality – that of the life, death and resurrection of Jesus Christ.

CHAPTER TWELVE

All shall have Partners

It seems more than reasonable to assume that the human race has always been interested in sex. It is also certain that the Christian Church has never been entirely sure what to make of this. In different places and at different times, the church has reflected every attitude from a visceral disgust at the physicalities of sex to an earthy realism which was virtually unshockable. In recent times, however, the church has been perceived solely in the role of killjoy. William Blake, in his well-known 'The Garden of Love' , sums up the whole matter to perfection:

I went to the Garden of Love,
And saw what I never had seen;
A Chapel was built in the midst,
Where I used to play on the green.
And the gates of this Chapel were shut
And 'Thou shalt not', writ over the door;
So I turned to the Garden of Love
That so many sweet flowers bore.
And I saw it was filled with graves,
And tombstones where flowers should be;
And priests in black gowns were walking their rounds,
And binding with briars my joys and desires.[11]

Is the church indeed called to replace flowers with tombstones or, indeed, to be nothing but 'death' to all sexual desire?

We do not need earnest surveys to make us realise that the entire social patterning of sexual activity in Ireland has changed out of all recognition in recent years. Fewer people are choosing

---
11. William Blake, 'The Garden of Love', *Poems* (Everyman Edition), J M Dent, 2004, p 36.

to marry rather than live in long-term partnerships. Marriage, should it take place, will normally occur – whether within a church service or not – after an extended period of time during which the couple have lived together. What are called 'second marriages' may not yet be the majority of all existing marriages, but re-marriage after divorce (or indeed a settled relationship with a new partner after divorce or separation) is today far from unusual. The percentage of children born out of what was once primly called 'wedlock' is rising fast.

In recent times in Ireland, those who acknowledge themselves as homosexual no longer conceal the fact and now, fully reasonably, seek a proper, open and legal recognition – certainly from the state and possibly from the church also – for relationships into which they have entered. Teenagers, including those in their early teens, are generally far more sexually experienced than in any Irish culture we have ever known. It might usefully be noted here, by way of *caveat*, that in other cultures – and indeed in an earlier Irish culture (where marriages would take place at a far earlier age than in present-day society) – sexual activity might indeed begin, or have begun, in the very early teens with full parental knowledge and consent. But has the church anything to say to any of the above, other than 'Don't do it', or else, 'Please do not seek to engage us on this, as we do not wish to be forced into attempting a coherent response'? Neither of these attitudes is worthy of any church which may seek any respect in the public arena and, even if the church cannot provide entirely satisfying answers, it should at least display a degree of honesty and openness in its approach to issues which are of such fundamental importance to so many of its most committed members. There are two principles which the church should consider carefully.

The first is that the church, in all its traditions, should learn to distinguish in its pronouncements between, on the one hand, its own discipline and practice and, on the other hand, what it may perceive as being for the common good of society. These are not necessarily coterminous. For example, it might surely be argued

ALL SHALL HAVE PARTNERS

that the institution of marriage is good for society at large and, in particular, for the proper care of children, without necessarily asserting that all marriages should be under the auspices of the church, or according to its practice and discipline. Secondly, the church must accept that its own attitude to sexuality through history is neither as consistent nor as coherent as it might wish to imagine or to claim. Indeed there is probably no better place to begin such a discussion on any of these matters than with this second point.

In the early Christian centuries, the only type of marriage, for Christians as for unbelievers, was that provided by civil practice. At the beginning of the fourth century, the synod of Elvira accepted explicitly that the marriages of baptised Christians might be celebrated in precisely the same way as for unbaptised pagans. Certainly, the church sought to bring a sense of Christian responsibility and pastoral care to the marriages of its members, but what made a marriage 'Christian' was the baptised status of the couple; it was not through any ceremony enacted by the church.

Marriage 'in the presence of the church' was simply non-existent in the early centuries of Christian history. It was probably only in the eleventh century that the church began to take any serious legal control over marriages. The essence of marriage, from the church's perspective, was that consent was given by both parties involved. The idea of the essential permanence of the marriage bond did, however, become bedrock to the church's definition of a proper marriage during the later mediaeval period. But it should still be emphasised that the due performance of a public formal ceremony inside or outside a church building was seen as very much of secondary importance. Throughout western Christendom, there was little uniformity in the matter. Nor was there anything approaching a standardised mores we take to be the Christian standard today. Even where the celebration of a mass accompanied the witnessing of a marriage, the newly-married couple might often be accompanied to the altar by their children! This indeed was an established method of legitimising one's children. It was not until the sixteenth century that the

Council of Trent decreed that marriages should be celebrated in the presence of clergy and witnesses in order to be considered as canonically valid.

Turning to the reformed traditions following the Reformation, here again there was no noticeable degree of uniformity. As with the mediaeval church, consent given freely (and, ideally, properly witnessed) was what made a marriage *valid*. In Britain it was only in the mid-eighteenth century that a church ceremony in the Church of England parish church was seen as any condition to the validity of a marriage. Particularly in more rural areas – throughout these islands, and until well into the twentieth century – there was no serious social shame attached to an informal marriage which had not been regularised within a religious ceremony. Because church and state in Ireland have combined for the past hundred and fifty years to produce a system under law which combines the civil and ecclesiastical aspects of marriage, the mistaken assumption has been created that the present arrangement has always been the reality.

The church has surely to consider again whether there should be a clear distinction between marriage as a civil institution, and the *blessing* – even when we consider there to be a sacramental covenant within this blessing – of a marriage between Christians. This latter is how matters are ordered in other countries and it would seem to accord far more to the practice of the Christian Church in the first half of its existence. At present, there is an utter confusion (which the Christian traditions have not sought to dispel) as to whether or not a wiynessed commitment given with consent between two adult people is fully and totally a marriage, one which should be regarded as a 'real marriage'. In this context, words such as *valid* or *canonical* may easily become more confusing than helpful.

Much of this discussion leads us towards a more fundamental issue. When the traditional moral code of the Christian tradition is rejected as being just 'religious morality' by a dismissive or contemptuous public, the Christian Church must take the courage to defend its stance by establishing that a religious moral code and common sense may not necessarily be at variance. Too often, morality is seen as something which claims its own intrinsic authority but has no other connection with a real world. In other words, people are told to behave in a certain way 'because God tells them to', and the fact that there may well also be common sense and social responsibility involved is ignored. The truth is that much of the Judeo-Christian teaching on sexual mores grew from the long experience of a community. Some of the codes of behaviour within the Hebrew Bible may seem restrictive, but they were not capricious, and were in fact often based on what was seen as the requirements of hygiene.

But there is more than medical or physical hygiene involved here. It may be certain that unrestricted sexual promiscuity leads to an increase in the incidence of sexually transmitted diseases (which are indeed on the increase in Ireland at present). But it might also be argued that a lack of any sexual restraint or restriction on sexual partnerships is also emotionally unhygienic. It is not merely a religious truth that an unlimited number of sexual partnerships creates an emotional immaturity which in turn makes it far more difficult for the individuals involved to engage in healthy relationships of any kind. It is also psychological truth. When sex becomes pleasure (which it most certainly is) but nothing other than bodily pleasure, it ironically becomes dehumanising. C S Lewis' delightful comment that humanity is related on the one hand to angels and on the other to tom-cats is undoubtedly true. However, it rather appears that traditional Christian moralism has tried to ignore the tom-cat in the hope of encouraging the angel. The church of today can only seek to raise the debate beyond tom-cat physicality if it first acknowledges that this physicality is in fact a crucial part of a reality which is itself fundamental to the human psyche. If the Christian Church wishes to say anything sensible on the matter (or, indeed, anything which will be listened to), it cannot be from the stunted, neutered and hypothetical perspective of a proverbial eunuch.

We might in similar vein argue that 'marriage', as the most

appropriate relationship in which to rear a family, is not merely restrictive 'religious morality'; it may be argued coherently that children will, for the most part, find it easier to grow happily and contentedly into maturity from within a settled and stable home family relationship. This does not mean that every marriage will be perfect or that every committed relationship outside marriage will *ipso facto* be unstable; one may speak only of social, psychological and even spiritual advantages to a public commitment in marriage to another individual.

Inevitably, there will be marriage relationships which become irrevocably destructive for whatever reason, and it may be that the only solution is that such a relationship should be brought to a conclusion. It is also undeniable that, over many generations, people (women in particular) have suffered from emotional and physical brutality within the marriage relationship, and have remained silent rather than suffer what they saw as the disgrace of concluding the marriage. But that need not of itself deny that marriage is a worthwhile institution, not merely for the individuals involved but also for 'the common good'. If the church can defend any traditional stance only on the grounds that it is true because the church has always preached it to be such (rather than because its truth also derives from the fact that – even today – it still happens to 'make sense') it will inevitably destroy its own case.

As people of every age now seek to castigate the church for its obsession with ordering people around, part of the delight in freedom from the restrictive code of the church will be the total rejection of anything and everything the church ever proclaimed. In short, the church must be able to defend its teaching on matters of sexual practice (as of everything else) not as mandatory because the church says so, but because it may well make sense in terms of public and private health.

A similar concern must be applied to the church's mind-set on homosexuality and on the nature of homosexual relationships. As the world of today finds the idea of any taboo – sexual or otherwise – less and less acceptable, there is a new spotlight on the whole church as it seeks to find a way to come to terms with a sexual nature which for centuries it stigmatised as inherently 'perverted'. In the first place, the word 'perversion' simply will not do. A pervert is someone who chooses a particular course of behaviour where other more appropriate options are available. We now know enough about sexual orientation to be certain that it is not purely a matter of choice. The Christian Church must be able to respond in some coherent way to those of its members – and we need to re-affirm here that the church *is* its members – who are homosexual (not as a lifestyle choice but as a given reality), who wish to express this reality sexually within a relationship, and who may also wish the church to give its blessing to this relationship. Many traditions within the church do not wish even to consider the matter. The tradition to which I belong, Anglicanism, is at present floundering amidst a Communion-wide debate on the issue. Indeed the debate is one which appears to be fragmenting the Communion itself.

Speaking from an entirely personal perspective, I find myself recognising that faithful relationships between those of the same gender may often be seen to bring goodness, hope, kindness and love into the lives of those around. It seems impossible to castigate such a relationship as intrinsically wrong. On the biblical basis of 'by their fruits you will know them', it is very difficult to categorise such individuals as being any more disordered than many of those who would smugly banish them. Indeed it seems to be sheer prurience for us to be greatly exercised as to what any particular homosexual couple might (or might not) be 'doing' sexually. Having said that, I would however add that my understanding of the scriptural tradition does not permit me to argue for any sustainable parallel between a relationship of those of the same gender, and the relationship of man and woman in marriage.

The New Testament, as is now well known, has little enough to say about homosexuality (and far less than it has to say about the permanence of marriage). The Old Testament is undoubtedly condemnatory of homosexual expression, but it condemns a great deal else that we would now accept as wholesome and good. It also approves other practices we today would regard as loathsome. Some of the contexts in which the prohibitions against homosexuality are expressed seem, to many scholars, to have as much to do (judging by their context in the text) with hospitality or with hygiene as with holiness of life *per se*. We must surely admit, without shame or undue defensiveness, that there are truths to which the Bible seems to have directed us, but only in the totality of its message. These are truths which have 'dawned on us' only over the passage of time. Both slavery and the subjugation of women are accepted (and actually encouraged) within the direct text of scripture itself, and yet most Christians today would see either of these as contrary to the essential spirit of Christ's teaching. We would argue that they were culturally conditioned by the context of the time, but that Christ was pointing us beyond this limitation, in all that he was and all that he taught.

There are no neat and tidy answers to the questions raised in a discussion on homosexuality, particularly when we ask further questions as to whether those entrusted with the leadership (and therefore also with the unity) of the church have the right to express their sexuality – if it happens to be homosexuality – within loving relationships. But there must be no 'no-go areas' for the church, and there are to be no questions which we judge to be too difficult, divisive or painful for us to ask. Many from outside the tradition have expressed approval for the fact that Anglicans – by however bumbling, discordant and gauche a means – are trying to discuss in public an issue which is deeply relevant to every Christian tradition. It may be at a terrible cost – in terms of unity and of mutual understanding within the Anglican Communion – but it may be a price that we must be ready to pay. We cannot avoid asking the question, seriously and humbly, as to whether the church's attitude to homosexuality requires re-definition. Sadly, while we seek to find answers, the entire argument becomes more polarised, the language of debate becomes more unrestrained and intemperate, and more and more people come to the unhappy realisation that the church is not for them.

But there is a final issue : do all need to have sexual partners? Post-Catholic Ireland, with a seemingly boundless prurience regarding sexual activity, appears unable to understand celibacy, or any willing renunciation of sexual activity. Celibacy and, indeed, chastity of any kind are seen as perversions or (at best) forms of escapism. Celibacy for the priesthood is a matter of discipline within the Roman Catholic tradition, and it would be impertinent for a member of another Christian tradition to pronounce on the appropriateness or otherwise of the discipline, other than to say that we all need to emphasise that it is precisely this, a matter of the internal discipline of one church tradition rather than the *esse* of priesthood itself.

Saint Paul's fated words that it is better to marry than to burn have done little to promote a mature understanding of either the institution of marriage or the voluntary renunciation of sexual activity. From the early centuries, sex became, for many people inside and outside the church, something regarded as existing only for the weaker elements in the church who had not the will-power to do without it. Marriage therefore became inherently an inferior lifestyle choice (to use the contemporary cliché) to celibacy. This has created a moral caste system which elevated those who had the strength of will and character to forgo sex, and demeaned those who wished to commit to another human being within a relationship which was sexual. In the current culture of an Ireland which wishes to vilify the church, that which cannot be understood – celibacy – must, it seems, be derided or even demonised. We must all share the blame for such a mindset. There is perhaps even an irrational and unwholesome fear of celibacy in a world which has become fixated on the sex-lives of all.

Underneath all of this is a truth which many wish to distort or deny. This is the reality that it is possible to have a fulfilling life without unbridled sexual pleasure or, indeed, any sexual activity at all. Many choose this latter path freely for the greater good of their vocation to ministry. Many others have no such choice; for some, an inability to have a sexual relationship is a fact of life. Those who are disabled in some way from birth, as with those for whom illness or accident have made having sexual expression an impossibility, are not to be regarded as being deprived of something without which life has no meaning or pattern. Ironically, in a culture which rightly wishes to esteem those who are in any way different from the majority, an exception seems to be made when it comes to the matter of sex. The continuation of life on earth depends on sex and hence on the pleasure which it gives, but an individual human life may well be complete and fulfilled without sexual activity.

Perhaps the church has for too long been insufficiently earthy about sex. It has in consequence made any of its pronouncements sound either puritanical or prurient. In the world in which we are set, the church has somehow to say unabashedly and plainly that the pleasures and fulfilments of sexual activity are indeed wonderful, but that sex is nevertheless not a sensible thing on which to fixate or to focus an entire life.

CHAPTER THIRTEEN

Saving Victims

At the very heart of the Christian proclamation is a victim – the crucified Christ. One of the hymns of Saint Thomas Aquinas, *O Salutaris Hostia,* proclaims this victimhood in majestic tones, 'O Saving Victim, opening wide the gate of heaven to all below.' In the Ireland of today, we are told often enough that we live in a victim culture, a society where many can understand themselves only as victims, if not as the individual victim of the intentional wickedness of others, then as the victim of their folly or carelessness. Can there be any connection between these different and differing victimhoods?

We should surely begin, however, with the reality that there are genuine victims aplenty all around us. There are those who have been exploited, ignored, abused and brutalised, either by society as a whole or by individuals in positions of control over them. Because we live in a culture where a sense of victimhood is a natural posture for those in trouble of any kind, we should never let that blind us to the actuality of injustice and cruelty within our society, which creates victims who are entitled to our intervention on their behalf. There are many in Ireland who are homeless. There are those who still sleep rough, and most definitely not 'by choice'. There is rural poverty on a wide scale. There is still widespread prejudice against those of a different colour, or of a different culture. Despite an economic boom through the 1990s, the extremes of wealth and poverty have expanded. At its best, the Judeo-Christian tradition places huge responsibilities on the shoulders of the righteous, that they will never avert their gaze from the destruction of the helpless. In this context, Jürgen Moltmann reminds us of precisely where it is that Christ is to be found. Taking the early Christian maxim, 'Where Christ is, the church is – *Ubi Christus, ibi ecclesia*', Moltmann points out that the twenty-fifth chapter of Matthew's gospel makes it clear that Christ is to be found among the most deprived of his brothers and sisters. In as much as we do good to the most neglected and degraded of his family, we do good to Christ himself. So, argues Moltmann, this is where the church is *in reality*, even if it does not acknowledge it. The church *is* where the poor are. Moltmann establishes what we might today call a twin-track approach. The church as the apostolate is the community gathered around the Word of God and the sacraments. This tells us *what* the church is. But if we wish to ask *where* the church is, we must look among the marginalised and the abandoned. It follows that the church does not carry charity to the poor, and nor does it do good to the underprivileged, because this is where the church already is. The church is those whom the world has abandoned. In a culture which stresses, more than has ever before been the case in this country, that individual achievement and material acquisition are the indicators of value, the church must understand where its true place is, alongside the victim rather than in thrall to the perpetrator of injustice.

But the question of victimhood has become something very much more complex in our society. Even those who are most obviously perpetrators of wrong seem more than capable of seeing themselves as more sinned against than sinning. To give one glaring and extreme example, many of those who have dealt with individuals found to have been guilty of the sexual abuse of children discover that the perpetrators of abuse may quickly consider themselves as the real victims. This may be either through an entirely unsustainable claim that the actions were consensual, or else that the perpetrator has suffered more than the abused individual, through the punishment, humiliation or loss of position that has been the consequence for him or her. Perpetrators may convince themselves that they have been unfairly treated by those responsible for them. Or they may see the problem as being within their own upbringing, and therefore as something for which they cannot be held responsible.

This is at one extreme end of a spectrum, but the generality remains that people have seemingly become unable to accept moral responsibility for their actions. This may in part be an over-reaction against a spiritual emphasis on sin which has for centuries been a central part of the message of the different Christian traditions, both catholic and reformed. Theologically it is simply impossible to remove the idea of human sinfulness from the Christian message, but because an emphasis on sin became the only picture that many carried from their childhood memories either of the confession box or of hell-fire sermons (from whatever tradition), sin and guilt have become as discredited as the church itself. This was underscored by the realisation that many of those in positions of responsibility within the Christian communities were themselves no less 'sinful' than those whom they or their predecessors had castigated for other sins. If this realisation is coupled with a growing individualism and hedonism within society, and the erosion of any notion that morality has an objective or transcendent framework, it is very simple to understand why people feel under less and less obligation to feel guilty about their behaviour. Further coupled to this is the wisdom of modern psychology that guilt may often be a pathological condition. Ironically, this does not mean that people now believe that there is no such thing as *blame*, or that no-one should ever be held accountable for things which have gone awry (far from it), but rather that they themselves need not feel encumbered by any sense of fault or failure.

A refusal to take any personal responsibility for wrongdoing is therefore linked, ironically, to the belief that one is somehow a *victim* of anything which goes wrong in one's life. Instead of suffering from an illness, we are now *victims* of cancer or heart disease. At present, we are witnessing a new concern with obesity as a dangerous condition for many in these islands. Whereas there are certainly those whose obesity is not a matter over which they have control (in that it may have been due to an underlying medical condition), these constitute a small minority. For most people, over-eating began as an individual's free choice. But yet we find the extraordinary need to find someone else to blame. If it is not to be fast food outlets that are directly to blame, then we must indict inadequate education on the importance of healthy eating habits. Individuals have thus become the *victims* of obesity. Some are not to blame for the fact that they are over weight. Most people must, however, take at least some responsibility for themselves and for their medical condition if they choose to eat too much. Even in less clear-cut areas of ill health, it seems that no-one is prepared to accept that there are times when it is our genes which are responsible for our condition and that *blame* is an inappropriate response. To regard ourselves as the victims of heredity is a very peculiar way of understanding existence on earth.

Medical practitioners are now forced to take out enormous insurance premiums in the face of a culture which assumes that there is always someone else to blame for an individual's illness. If one cannot blame a bad diagnosis, there is always the possibility that poor surgery or incorrect medication may be held as blameworthy for the fact that one has become a *victim* of pain or of less than perfect health. Whereas there are undoubtedly incidents of medical carelessness which require attention and redress, there is also an underlying and disturbing aspect to the mindset that seeks a scapegoat for every medical setback. In a society which has lost its sense of the eternal, vulnerability and even mortality itself are no longer seen as givens. No-one can come to terms easily with the reality of terminal illness or even of incapacity. But the refusal to believe that one may actually be ill, but without this illness being somehow the 'fault' of another human being, reveals an immaturity and an escapism which is as damaging to the soul of society as it is to individuals. It is a symptom of a deep unease within society that we cannot accept pain or mortality, without believing that this is the fault of someone else. Now that we can no longer blame God, it is fellow humans who are to be held responsible.

This deep-seated unease within Irish society today, with its concomitant refusal to believe that we are not inevitably the victims of others' incompetence or carelessness, has visibly infected the life of Christian communities. To express it directly, many clergy today believe themselves to be the victims of their own parishioners. In some cases, it is the sense that they are being constantly evaluated and that their ministry is being judged in terms of 'value for money'. Clergy may therefore often feel under pressure to undertake the obvious and more visible aspects of ministry, rather than the less noticeable but no less essential tasks. As a corollary, parishioners in many communities may often feel that they are not getting the service they deserve for their financial input into the funds of the community. If a priest or pastor does not have a particularly graceful manner, the parishioner may indeed feel that they are being treated with indifference or contempt. The point is not that this is less than serious, but rather that it appears to be a new situation. Clergy of previous generations found that they could cope with demanding parishioners; parishioners found that they could live – however uncomfortably – with eccentric clergy. The cry for accountability, and the apparent need within every area of community to cast self as *victim*, has made the relationship between clergy and people in many Christian communities both more uneasy and, unquestionably, less relaxed and settled.

In the wider context, a question must inevitably arise in the modern mind as to where precisely 'being a victim' begins and ends. Many believe that they have been made a victim, not by what they have suffered, but by what they have witnessed happening to others. In some cases we may indeed see this as a reasonable assessment. The loving self-sacrificing carer of a relative who is dying slowly and painfully of a wasting illness will indeed suffer terribly, and will be scarred for many years after their loved one has died. They are collateral victims of another's distress and pain. Others believe themselves to be *victims* when they have witnessed road accidents, or have found themselves by chance at the scene of gruesome events in which people have died horribly. Those, for example, who were present at disasters at sporting events have rightly needed professional help in coming to terms with what they have seen and heard, but we must ask the question as to whether we should use the word 'victim' as loosely as we often do. Much can be trivialised and distorted by too careless a usage. It is surely significant that those who devote their lives to the care of others in distress rarely speak of themselves as victims of what they encounter. They can see only the distress of others. It is unknown, for example, to hear an aid worker returning from Africa referring to himself or herself as being a victim of terrible sights. Their sympathy and righteous indignation are directed to the plight of others. Similarly those who nurse the terminally ill in hospices often need to take temporary leave because such work is, of its very nature, emotionally exhausting and draining, but (in almost every case) they will then return to the fray and continue their work of care and support without undue fuss or sense of grievance.

Without denigrating in any way the distress people may feel in witnessing the distress of others, whether physical or emotional, we must surely accept that the culture of Ireland today is more self-obsessed than ever before. Men and women must surely learn, as they would have accepted naturally until recent times, that they are not, as individuals, the real centre of all existence. The suffering of others is terrible to witness. But the first question to come to mind must surely be, 'What can I do to make this better?' rather than, 'How is this affecting me?' The loss of a sense of community and, by extension, of an instinctive sense of responsibility for the plight of others has created a dangerous and noxious emphasis on the self.

Because of an increasing consciousness of victimhood as universal, 'being a victim' has also ensured a place on the public stage. The claim that one has been victimised will attract a great deal more publicity and public interest than any claim that one is being extremely well treated. Part of this is sheer prurience. There is something within the human psyche which is, to put it crudely, energised by the thought of disaster striking another.

But there is another aspect to the matter - because there is a victim, there is also someone to blame. There are indeed often people to blame for the damage they have inflicted on others, but the demands for vengeance on the person to blame may too easily become disproportionate and deeply unwholesome. The biblical image of the goat being driven into the wilderness - the original 'scapegoat' - to atone for the sins of the people, springs readily to the imagination. Because people seem satisfied to be perceived as victims, there is a concomitant requirement to find villains and to demonise them. There is an increasing frenzy within Irish society to identify those who make victims of others, and then to make them suffer in turn, if not financially then with the ignominy of public disgrace.

The term schadenfreude has no direct parallel in the English language. 'Pleasure at the disgrace of others' is probably the best translation. Where there are perceived victims, there are perceived perpetrators and the vilification of these offenders becomes a pleasure for the onlookers. It is very primitive and very dangerous. People are encouraged to think of themselves as fundamentally 'good', if they are able to luxuriate in the exposed guilt of others. And so the entire business of schadenfreude becomes a commercial proposition. Newspapers sell more copies if they are able to indulge the reader's lust for the shaming of others. Television programmes attract more viewers (and this also has commercial rewards) if 'naming and shaming' is on the agenda. The media have done a huge service to Irish society in shining a bright spotlight on dark murky places where appalling evil was being done to the weak and powerless (not least by the Church itself). But what begins as a crusade for good may itself become twisted. It would be utter naivety not to grasp the truth that commercial considerations are very much part of decision processes as to what constitutes news in any of the media. News is what is presented to the public as news. News is what will sell. Those who consider themselves victims of the media may not always be self-deluded. Irish society desperately needs a free press. There must be a media free from any censorship imposed by church or government, but it must also be a media free from the commercial considerations which will pander to the less wholesome aspects of the human psyche, not least schadenfreude. Juvenal's famous question, 'Quis custodiet ipsos custodes? - Who will guard the guardians themselves?' – must be applied to every aspect of society. Who will turn the spotlight on the less savoury aspects of the media? Who will be allowed to view what is uncovered by such a searchlight?

There is no doubt that the Church of post-Catholic Ireland sees itself as a victim. Indeed it views itself as a victim of many difference forces. First and foremost, it believes that it has been victimised by the media. This perception is worth a little further investigation. Undoubtedly the Irish media have given the Church - the entire Church, north and south - a harsh interrogation in recent years. The Church needs to ask itself honestly if this is not deserved. In Northern Ireland, the reformed traditions in particular have been cross-examined by the media as to the degree to which they have fostered sectarianism. Sectarianism is of itself an evil thing, but when it divides an entire society and foments violence (even if not directly sponsoring this violence), it becomes satanic in its impact. Until the reformed traditions are able publicly to accept this fact, and to recognise further that systemic sectarianism has created damage both to the proclamation of the Christian faith and to the nature of society in Ulster, the interrogation will continue.

Further south, there has been an equally hostile scrutiny of the Church by the media. There is no doubt that many people throughout the island are genuinely sickened by the unfolding revelations of child abuse in institutions under the control of the Roman Catholic Church. We have to ask the honest question as to whether the matter would have been exposed so vigorously or investigated with such energy if the media had not given such publicity to the scandals. There is a sense in which the Church should even feel gratitude that nothing it says or does will any longer be above scrutiny, even if at times it seems that the scrutiny is intimidating and menacing. What has also been revealed however is that there is, beneath the surface, a great deal of antagonism towards the Church which is not entirely related to specific scandals but which had far more to do with resentment of what was seen as the control the Church exercised both over its members and within the government of the state. The exposure of scandals gave a free rein to a rage which had been waiting for the opportunity to explode. Again, one may only say that if the essential truth of the criticism is acknowledged, it becomes easier to confront the assaults on everything the Church stands for, or has ever stood for.

The reformed traditions in the south have far less for which to cry foul. They have for the most part been given the status of a rare and exotic species which should be preserved from extinction if at all possible. Most criticisms of them in the public arena have been directed more to their general air of complacency and a bland refusal to become embroiled in controversy of any kind, both of which have been the characteristics of a minority grouping which sets an absurdly high store on the importance of its own survival.

But, to return to the point at which this essay began, can there be any common thread between a human victimhood which is at least partially deserved, and the Victim who stands at the very centre of the Christian faith? Christ is portrayed through the entirety of the Christian history and practice as a victim of injustice, hatred, and, indeed, of all human wickedness. There has been a powerful tradition within the Christian Church since earliest times which sees victimhood as something for disciples to embrace. The witness of Christian martyrs over the centuries has enriched the proclamation of Christ by the Church. The word martyr even means witness. To be a witness is to be a martyr and hence a victim, in one way or another, but the apparent universality of victimhood in the culture of today means that we have to think far more carefully about how we define the victim. If an individual's suffering is in fact the price of his or her own folly, carelessness or self-indulgence, the word victim is surely inappropriate. But if we set Christ as the model of true victimhood, certain characteristics emerge. The victim is someone who does not deserve, in any sense, that which has been meted out to him or her. This may of course be a matter of degree, and a victim (particularly an institution or a community) may well be responsible to some extent for what has been inflicted, but not to the level of suffering or pain that has been exacted. But the authentic victim is predominantly innocent. And within any human society the issues of truth and justice must therefore be central. True victims are entitled to true justice. Authentic justice, however, is not only calm and deliberate in its operation. It must also be impartial and dispassionate. It is not governed by the possibilities of financial gain or by schadenfreude. True justice for victimhood must never be influenced by populism, by that which the public would like to see happen, or – worse again – by that which the public is artificially induced to believe it should like to see happen. Heaven's gates are not so easily opened, and the church must have the courage to make the authentic connections, but also to deny all bogus connections with that which is the ultimate meaning of all true and salvific victimhood, the Cross of Christ.

POSTLUDE

Grace with Everything

One of the most familiar stories in the gospels is that of Christ's rescuing of his disciples as they find themselves in danger on the Sea of Galilee, their boat sinking and their nerve shredded. It is told in different ways within the gospels. Matthew's version of the story (in chapter fourteen) tells of how Christ told his disciples to cross the lake as he went into the mountains to pray. As they battle against the storm in the middle of the night, they see him coming towards them over the waves. Simon Peter, never a man to be outdone or upstaged, asks if he may walk across the water to Christ. Christ tells Peter to come to him but, as he becomes more and more aware of the danger, Peter begins to sink. Christ intervenes to save both him and the other disciples in the boat, while also confronting them with their lack of faith. His presence in the boat, as he boards it, brings an immediate stillness, quiet and reassurance.

Not surprisingly, the story has gripped the imagination of the church from the days of the earliest Christians. Not only is it a spellbinding story in its own right, but it carries also a wealth of symbolism. The church has, from very early Christian times, been represented as a boat or ship. The account of the rescue of the disciples may be understood as conveying also the image of Christ ready to rescue the church as, facing oblivion, it proves incapable of saving itself. Christ is able to rescue the church at its most fearful and vulnerable, but not in its vanity and pride. The additional story about Peter was a reminder of the fragility of human faith in times of stress and terror, and is perhaps a reference also to the sin of hubris, as pride in one's own prowess leads inexorably to humiliation.

As the Irish church seeks to work for its own future, it would do well to remember this gospel story. There is certainly no doubt but that the church must take responsibility for what it has been, must learn from its past and its present, and must dramatically change its ways if it is to move with any confidence into any future. Equally, however, it must surely remember that it does not have the ability of itself to do anything other than sink. It is not an empty piety to emphasise that the church must now throw itself not only at the mercy of the people of Ireland but also at the mercy of God if it is to recover its stability and re-establish its purpose. All the smart public relations exercises in the world cannot save the church. Only the grace of God will effect that transfiguration. The church must, therefore, place itself at the disposal of grace.

Grace requires from us first the admission that we cannot in our own strength and pride make of the church what God calls it to be. We must therefore learn to pray as the church, not as competing fiefdoms or squabbling cousins. Worship has always been the true foundation of the church and it is through worship alone that the church is given the perspective, humility and strength to continue its mission. For as long as Christians worship in competition with one another or with complacency at the present state of affairs, God's grace cannot intrude. Grace demands surrender and the admission of need. It is only in worship that the awareness of failure can become apparent and that the cry for help can be made with integrity. The gospel story of a near sinking on the Sea of Galilee reminds us that Christ may indeed *almost* let his disciples drown. It is only when the disciples show an awareness of their own insufficiency that Christ can act, decisively and effectively. And it is only when the church confesses its own inability to restore itself that a restoration may come through the grace of God. This cry for help must begin in worship which is truthful, self-effacing, and unified. As the plight of Simon Peter reminds us, 'solo runs', particularly when they are accompanied with vanity and self-assurance, are destined for disaster.

POSTLUDE

Those first disciples wished to get to the other side of a lake in safety. The church today wishes to hand something worthwhile on to those who are to carry the light of the gospel further. What would that vision be? If we look back to the earliest church – and it is of course naïve to imagine that we could ever totally replicate that church in the society of today – we see that its strength lay, not in a powerful centralised structure but in the vibrancy of local communities. The strength of the Christian Church will always be in the way it worships and behaves in its localised setting. If local church communities are magnetic in the authenticity of their worship, immediacy of fellowship and impact upon the world around, people will wish passionately to belong. This is particularly true in a culture which has lost its sense of community and of belonging. Central church structures are there only to support and to empower local church communities, not to browbeat or police them. In the world in which we live, we may assume that there will be a continuing need for central organisational structures for the church, but the principle of subsidiarity must pertain. It is important that the church avoids spiritual and doctrinal fragmentation, but it is equally important that the church realises precisely where its future, and the future of the proclaimed gospel lies – in the living and local community.

The church must indeed have its vision for the future, but if it moves forward purposefully yet humbly, listening as well as proclaiming, its vision will inevitably change with the progress of its pilgrimage. We do not have to possess a unified vision of what the end of the road will look like before we begin the journey. In his autobiography, the great violinist Yehudi Menuhin gave us a remarkable parallel from the world of music. He writes of the temptation to see, as two distinct things, the ideal of what the music should sound like, and the practice required to attain that ideal. He says that they are not distinct. The activity of practising – of doing – will itself expand the vision. Sometimes, he writes, he would find his fingers suggesting ideas that listening and study had not prompted. This is true, Menuhin goes on to suggest, of human endeavour also. There are ideas that are stretched by practice. And so, he concludes, 'vision hauls practice upwards, and in rising, practice pushes further the boundaries of vision'. For us, the doing of Christ-like behaviour by the church may well push further the boundaries of the vision of a future church. There is a time for defining the vision, but there is also a time when we have to stop talking or writing and start practising. By all means let the faithful remnant possess a vision of where they wish the Irish church to be in ten or twenty years time, but let them possess also the discernment to realise that the vision for the future church will certainly be changed, along a journey which is travelled in the companionship of friends and of Christ. For that is what grace does.